A walk around Paris

Robert Ornig

"Paris is the only city in the world where starving to death is still considered an art."
Carlos Ruiz Zafon

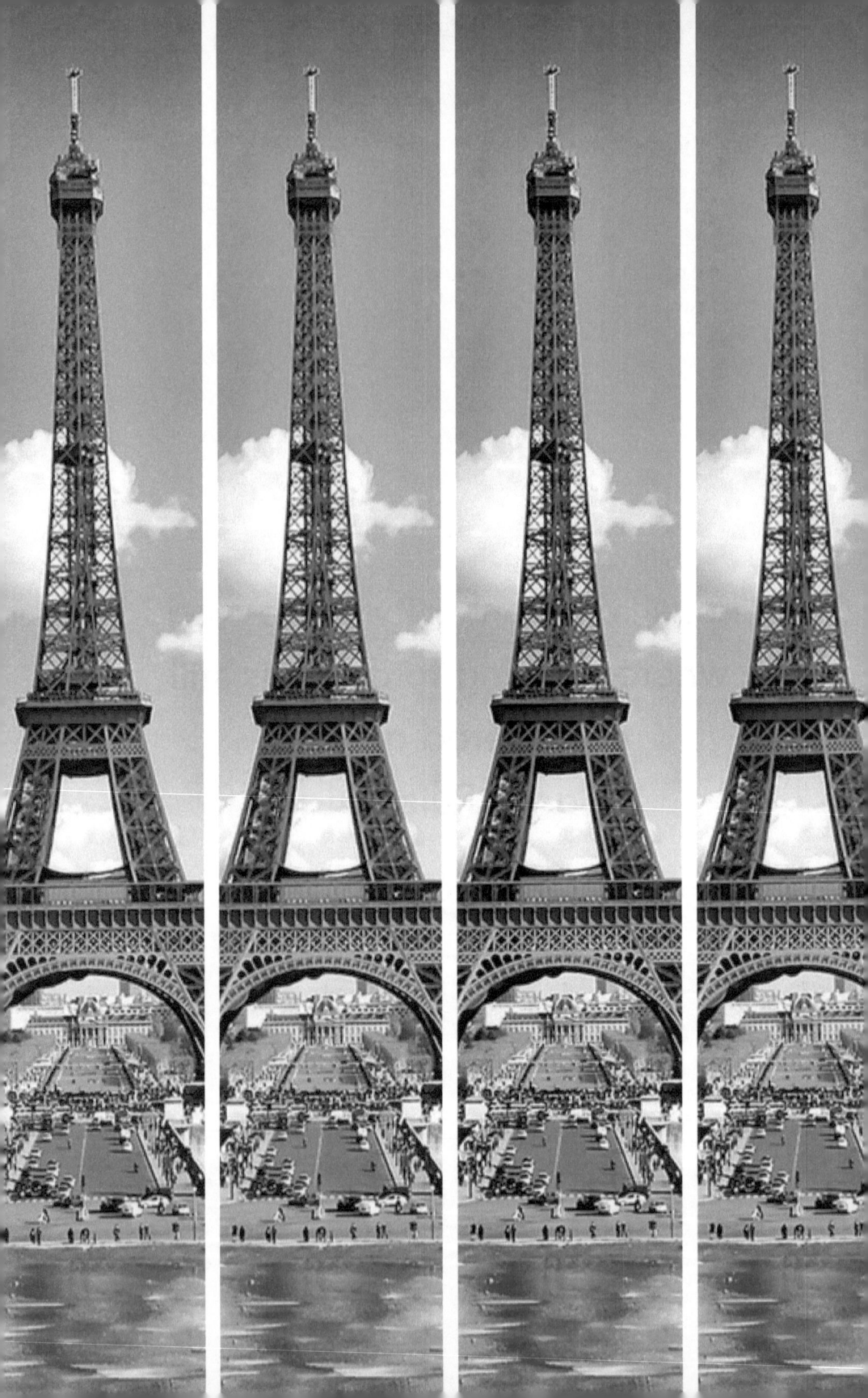

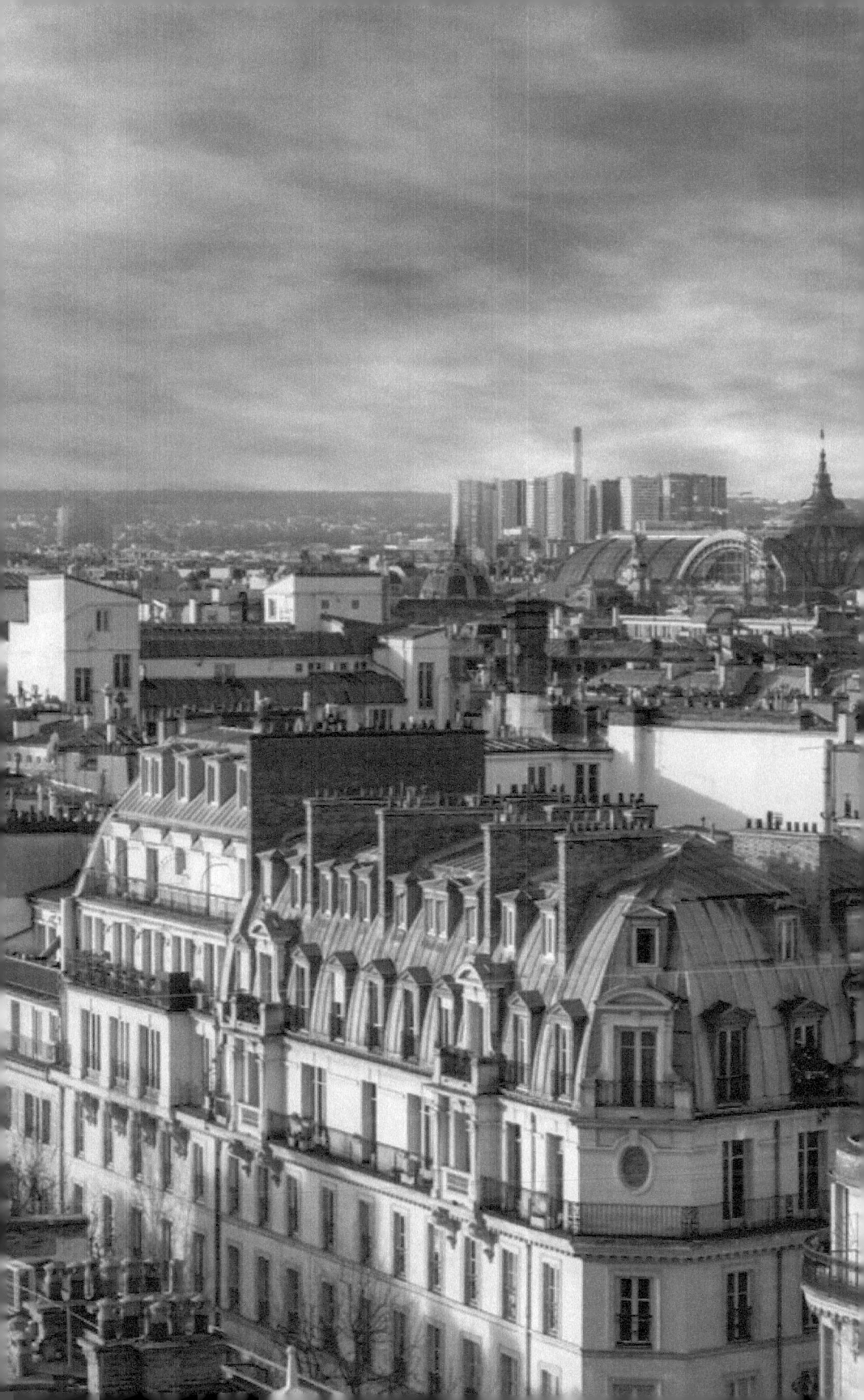

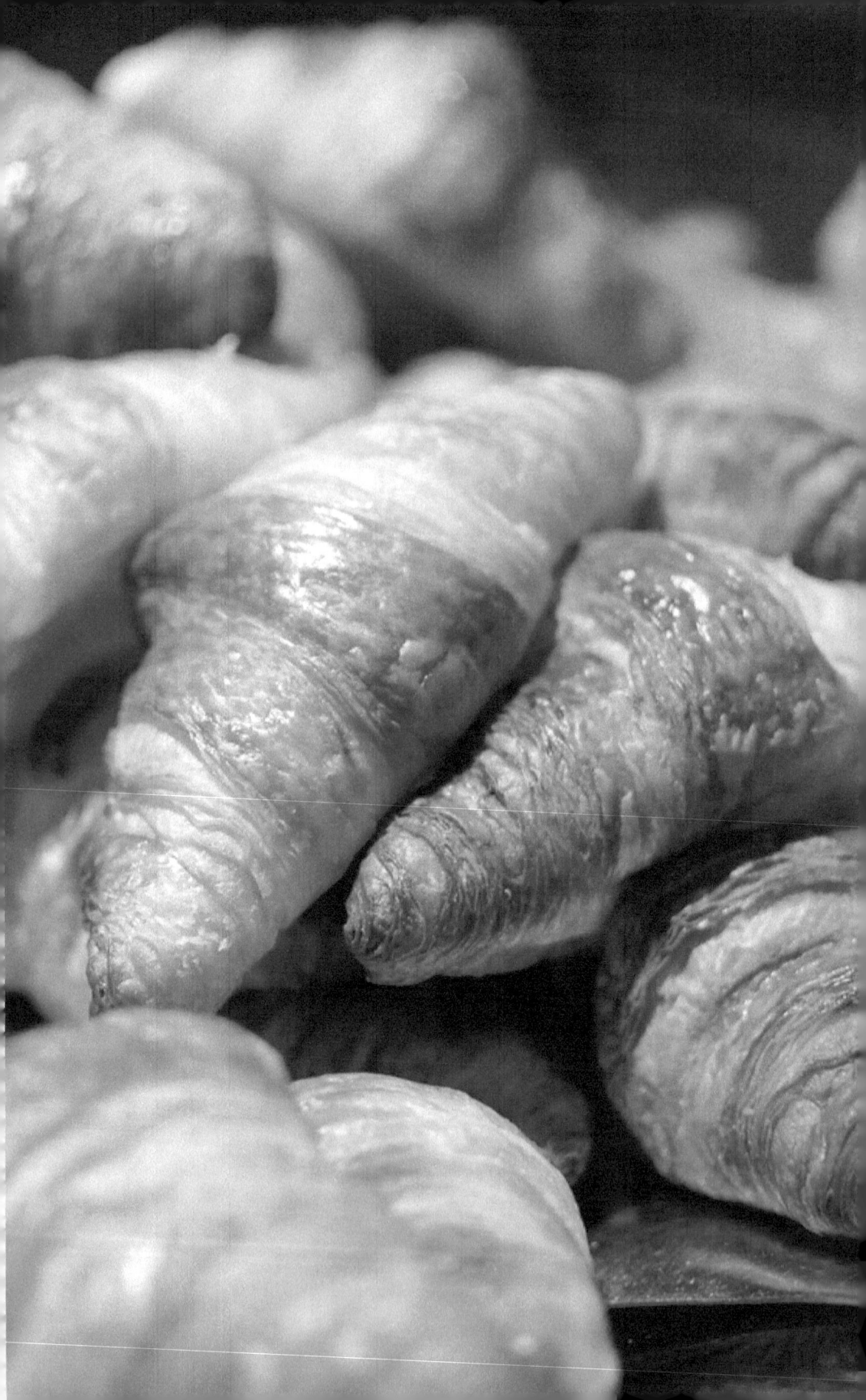

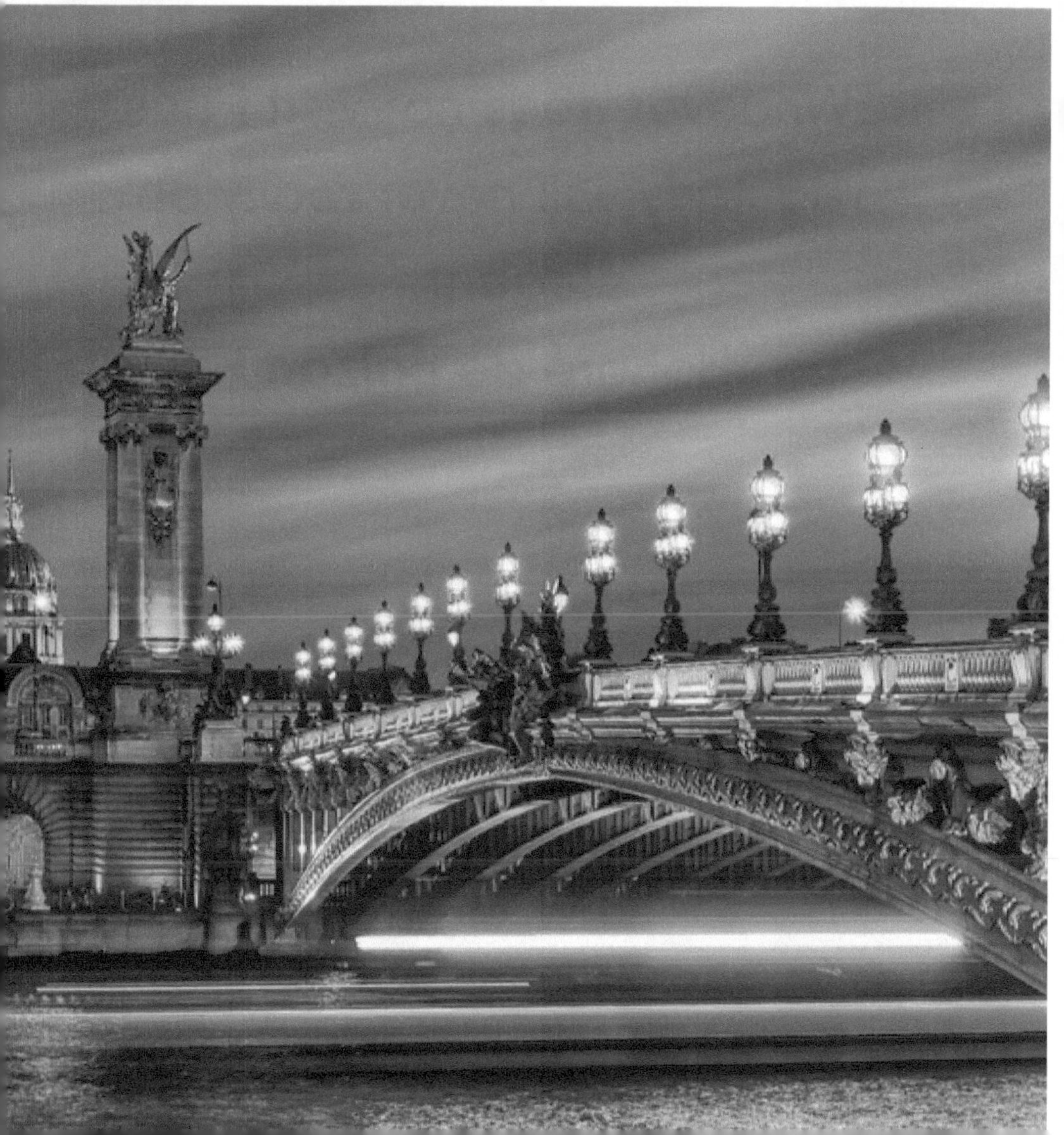

"Whoever does not visit Paris regularly will never really be elegant."
Honoré de Balzac

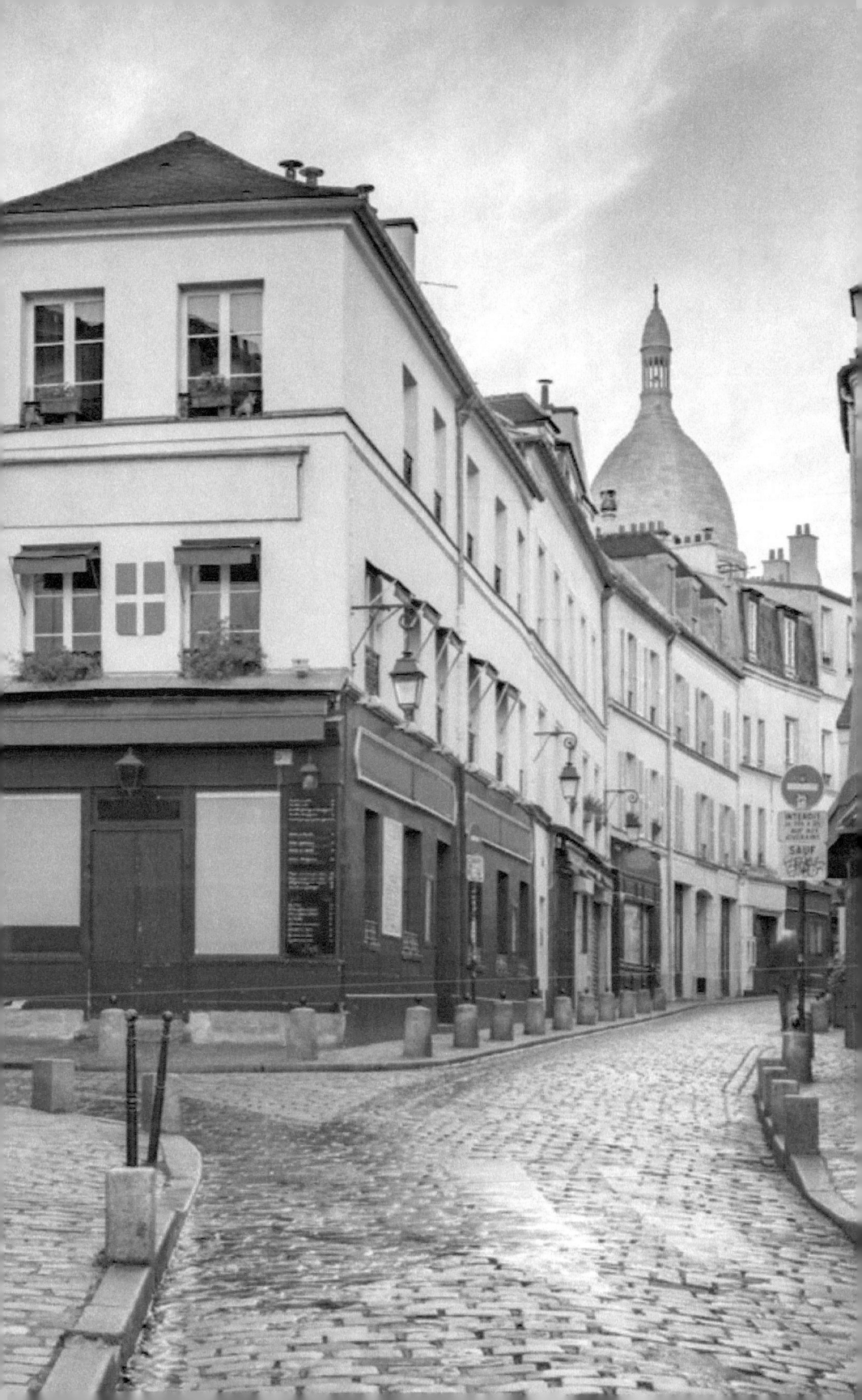

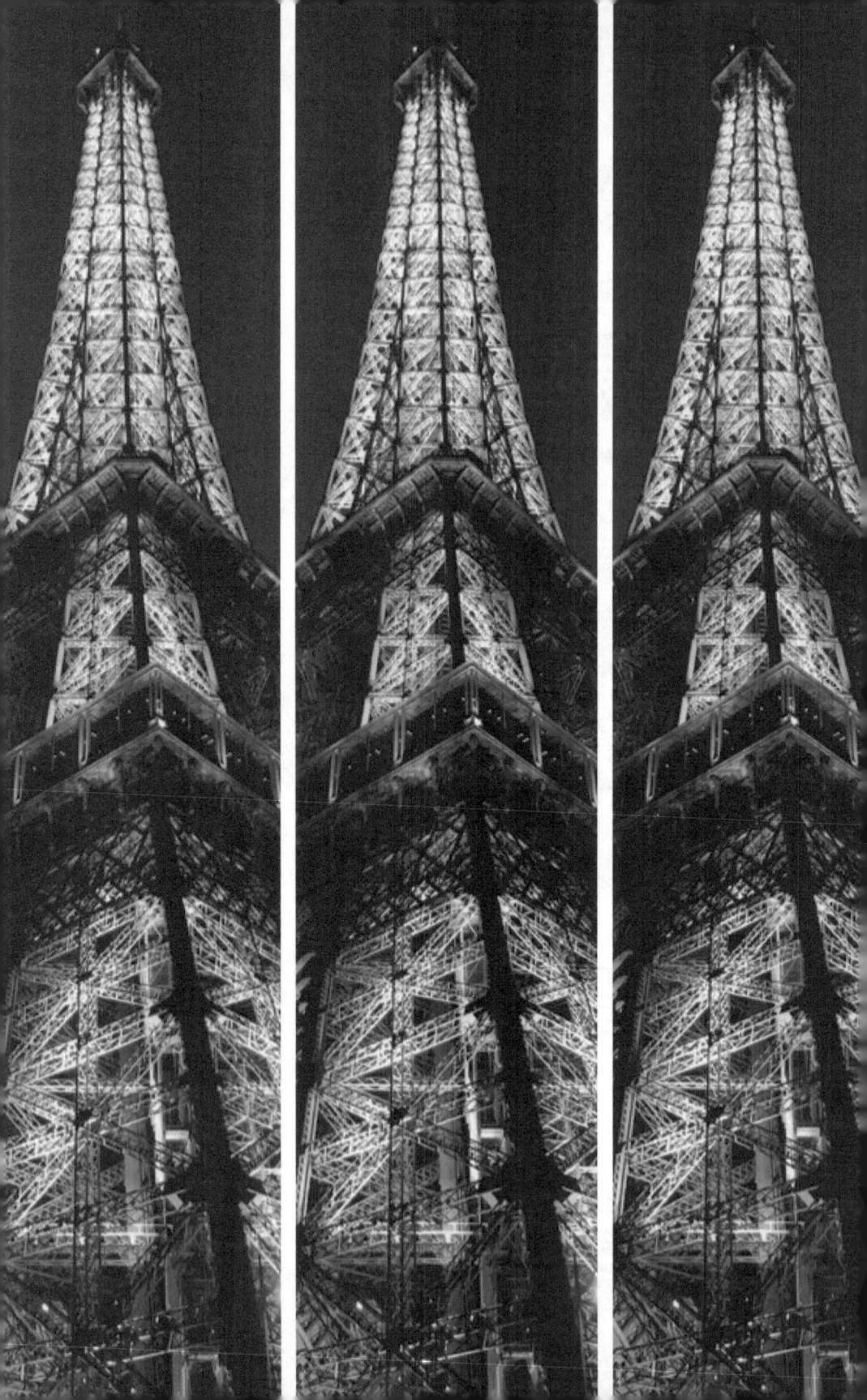

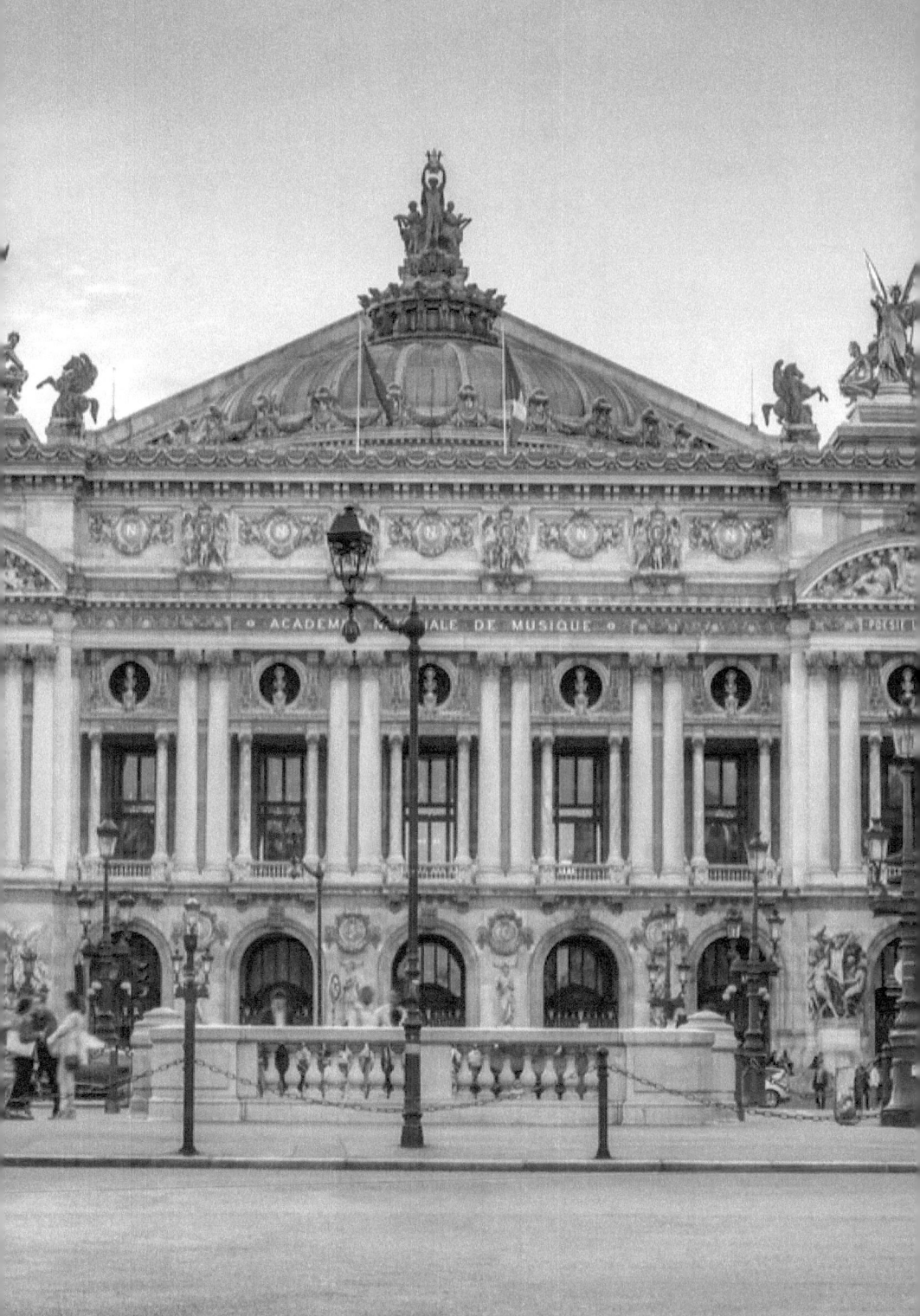

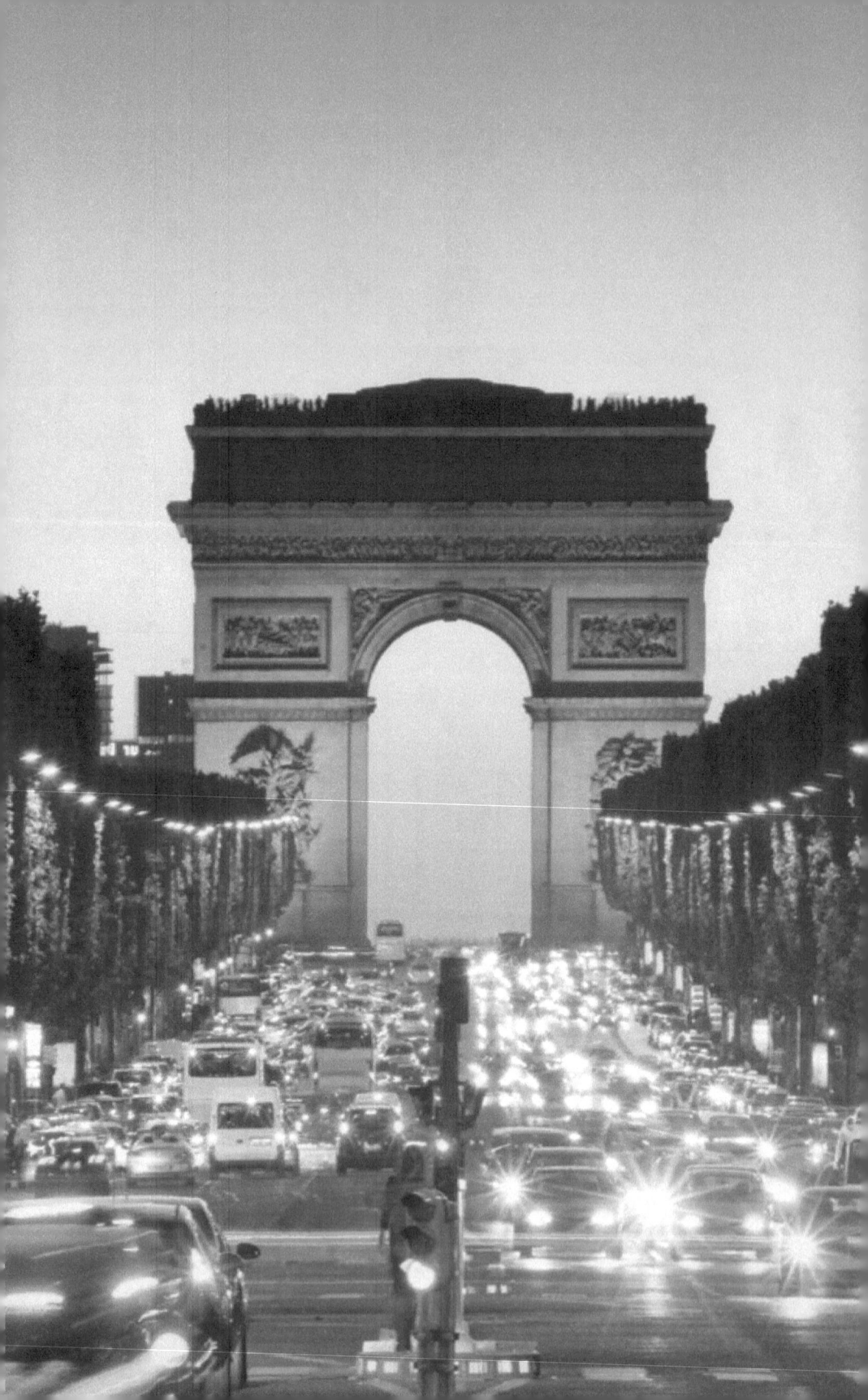

"Secrets travel fast in Paris." – Napoleon Bonaparte

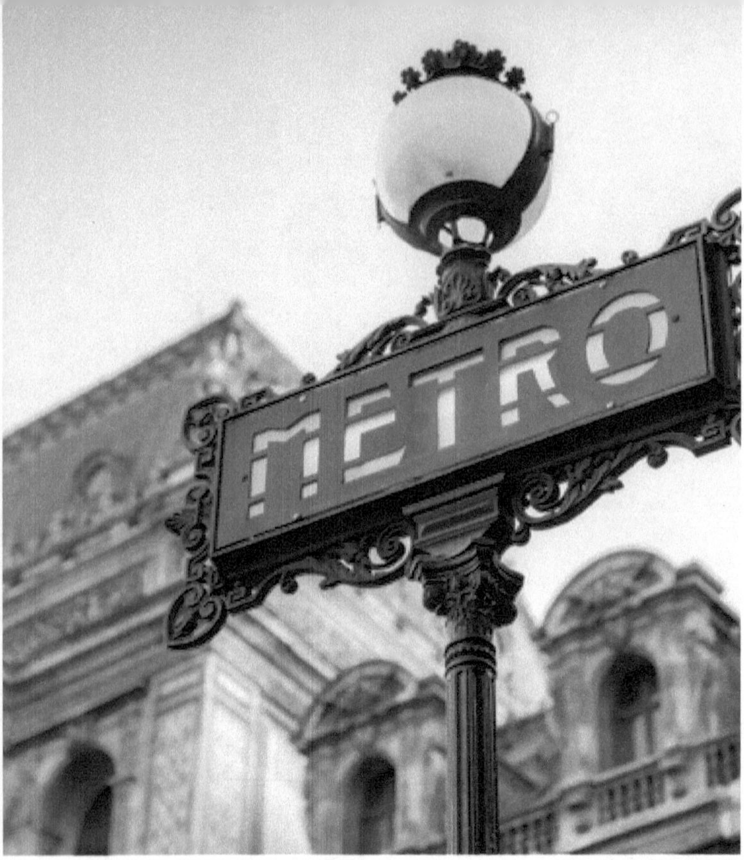
METRO
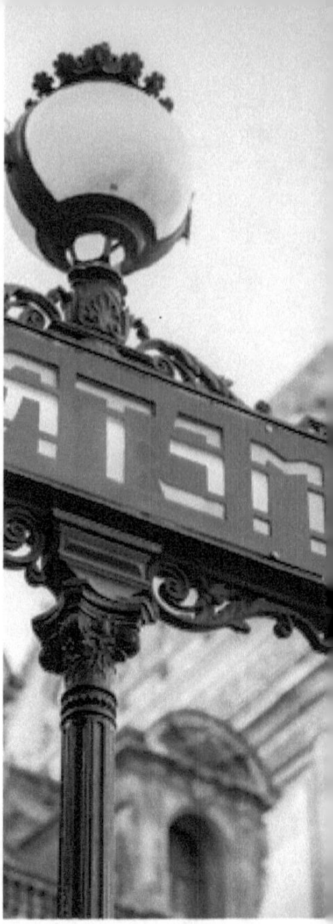
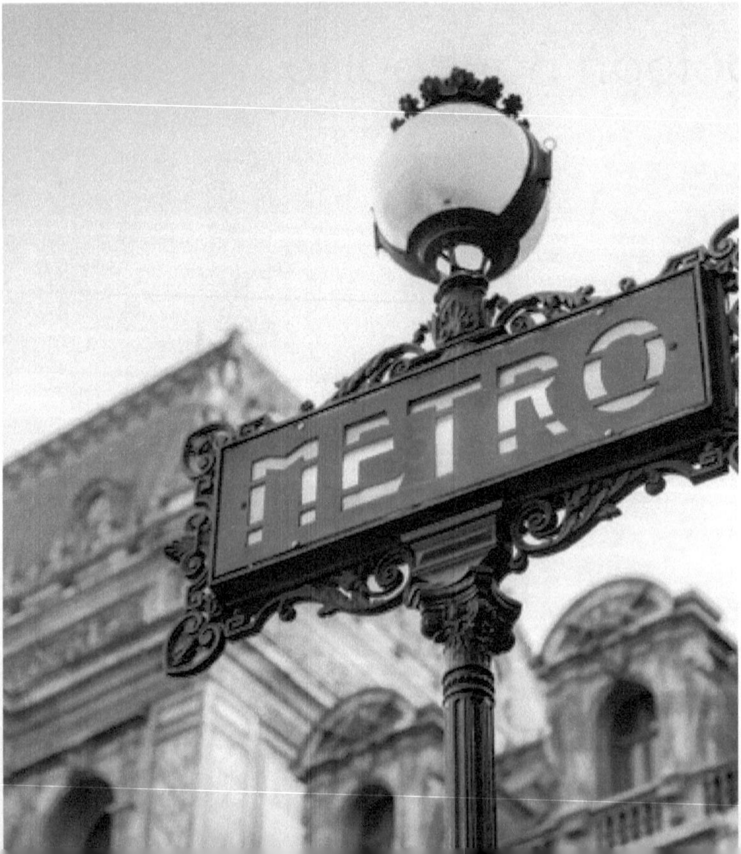
METRO
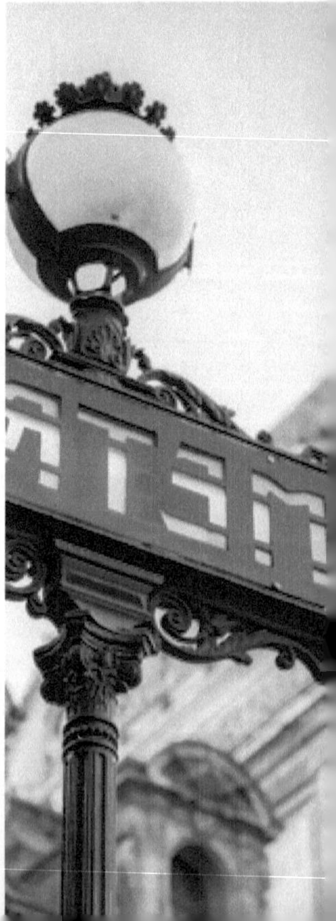

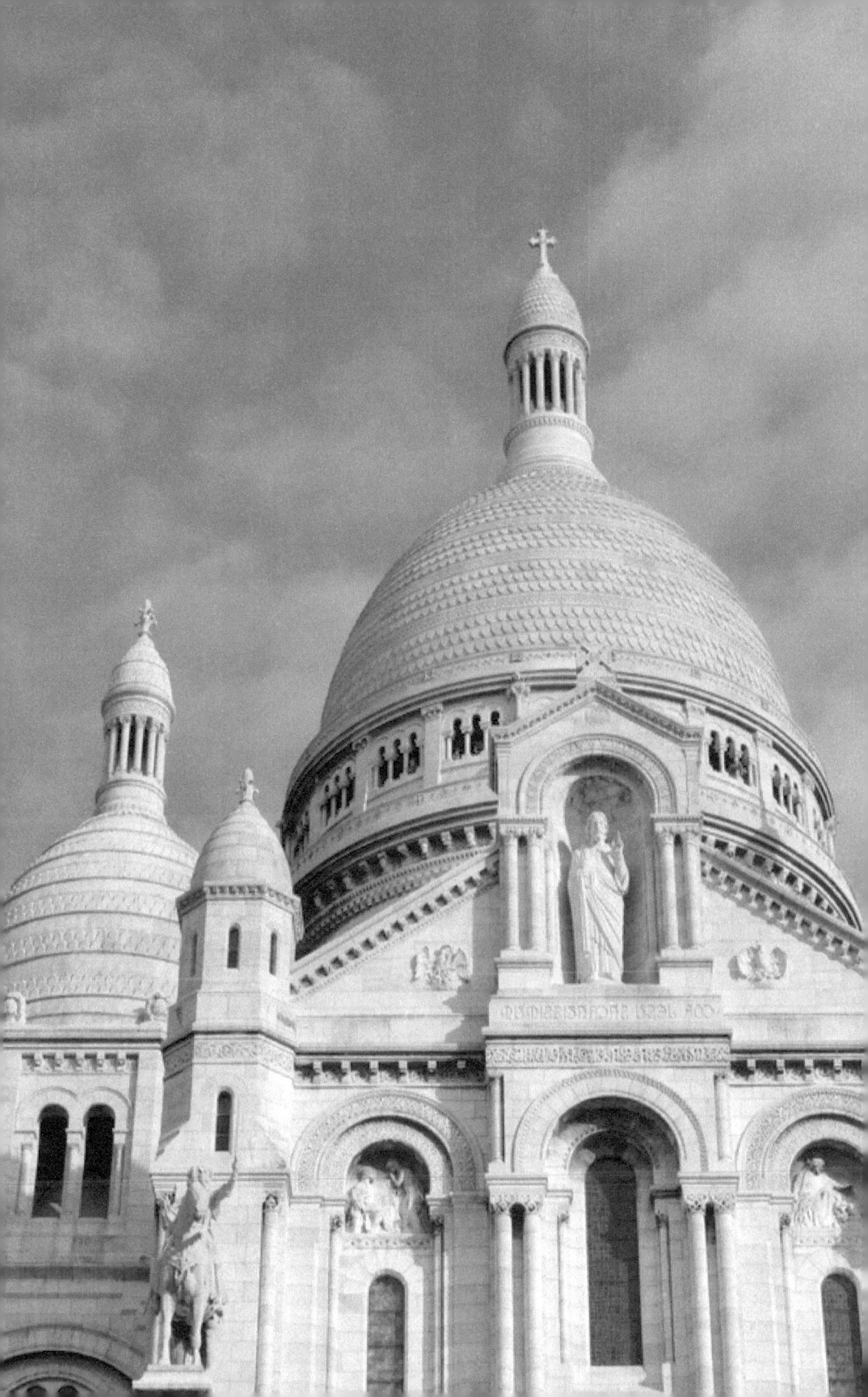

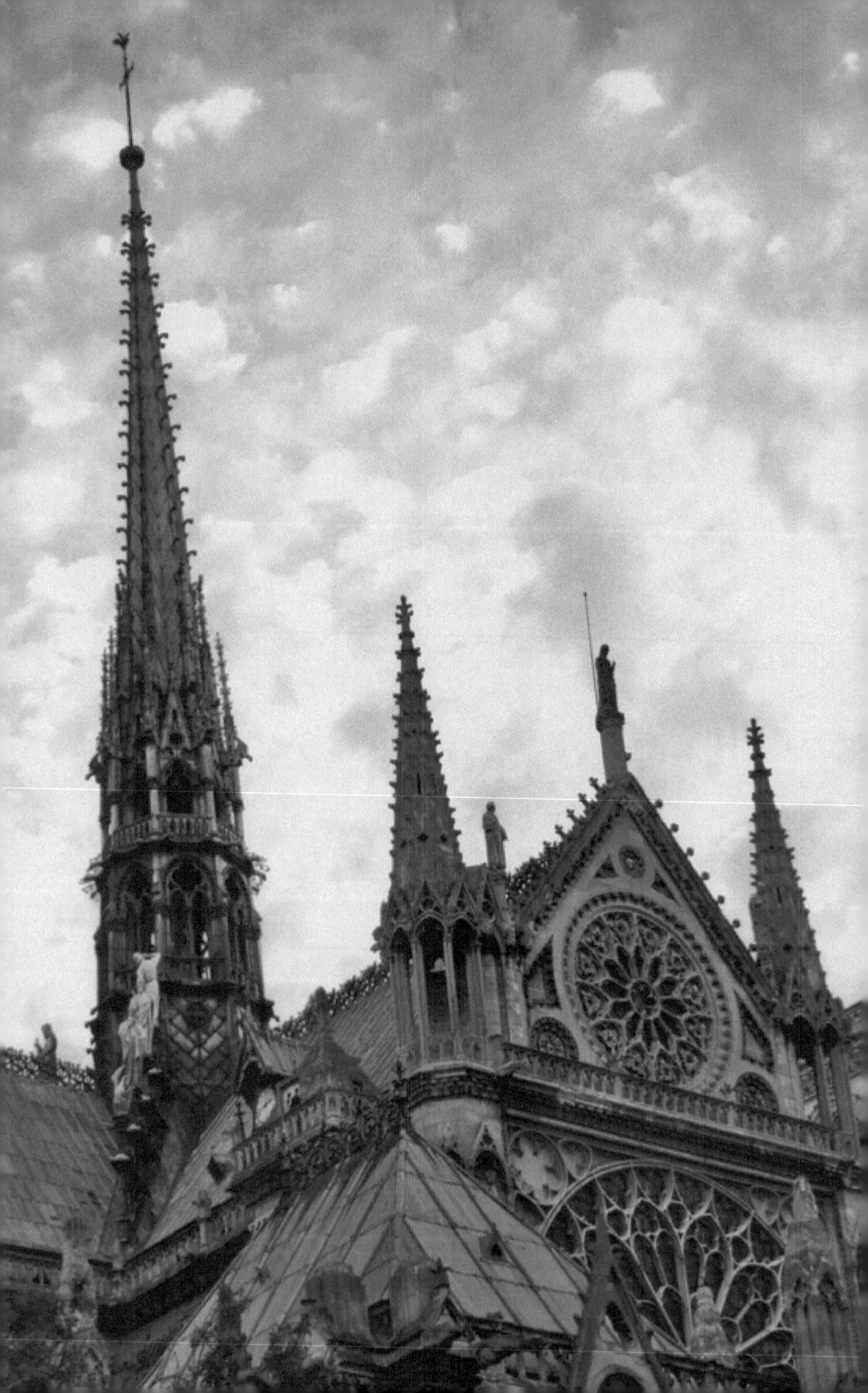

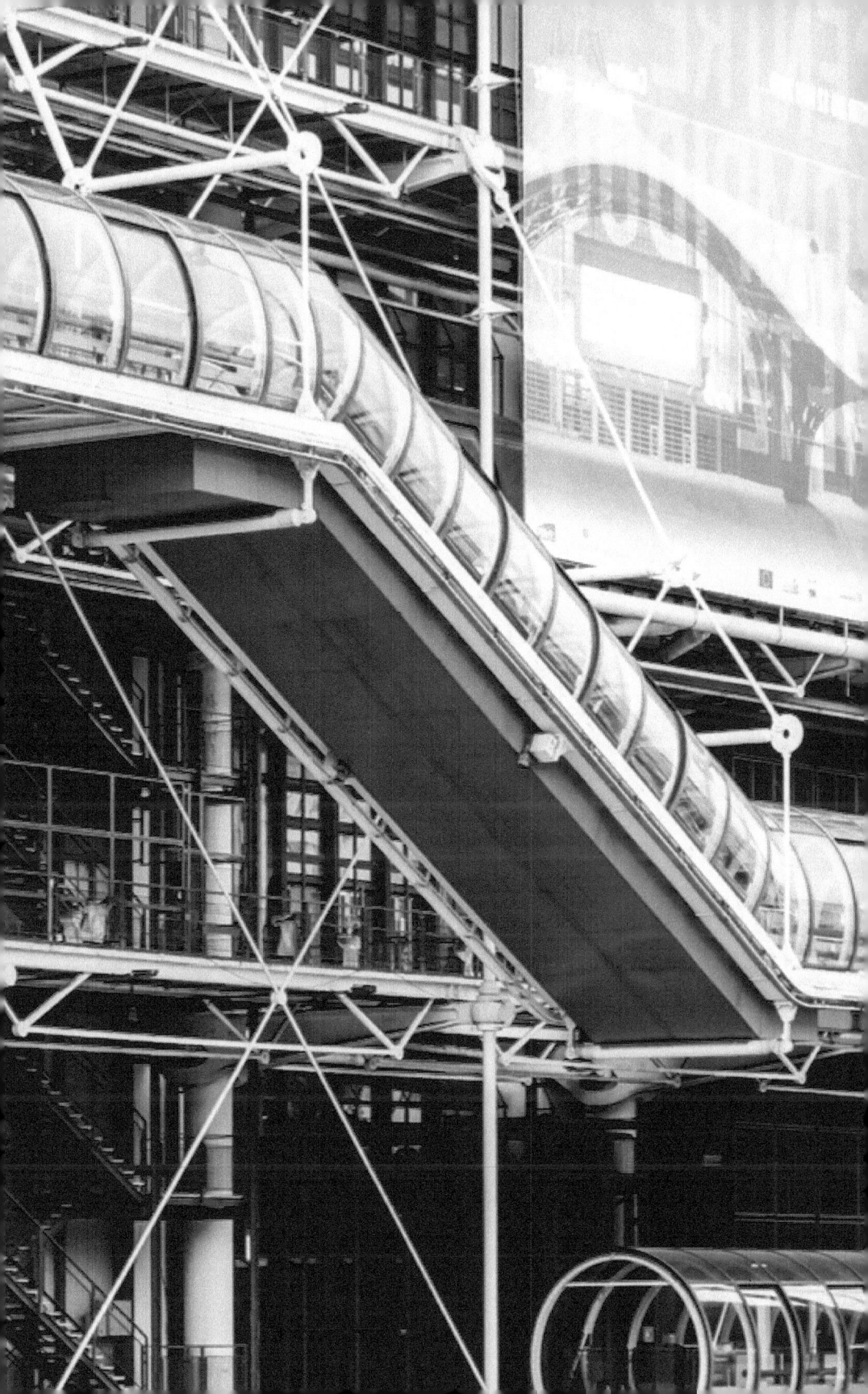

"An artist has no home in Europe except in Paris." -Friedrich Nietzsche

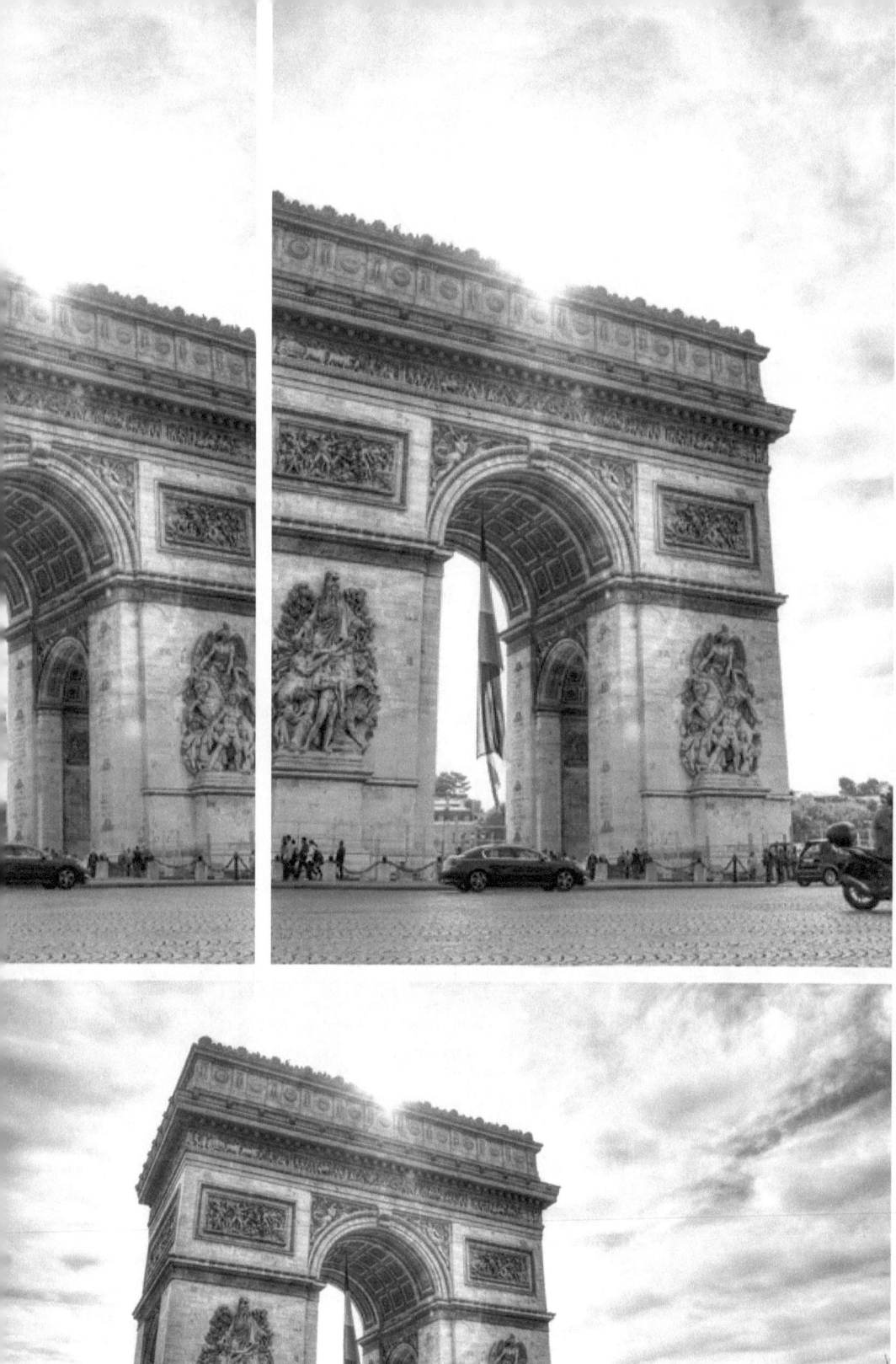

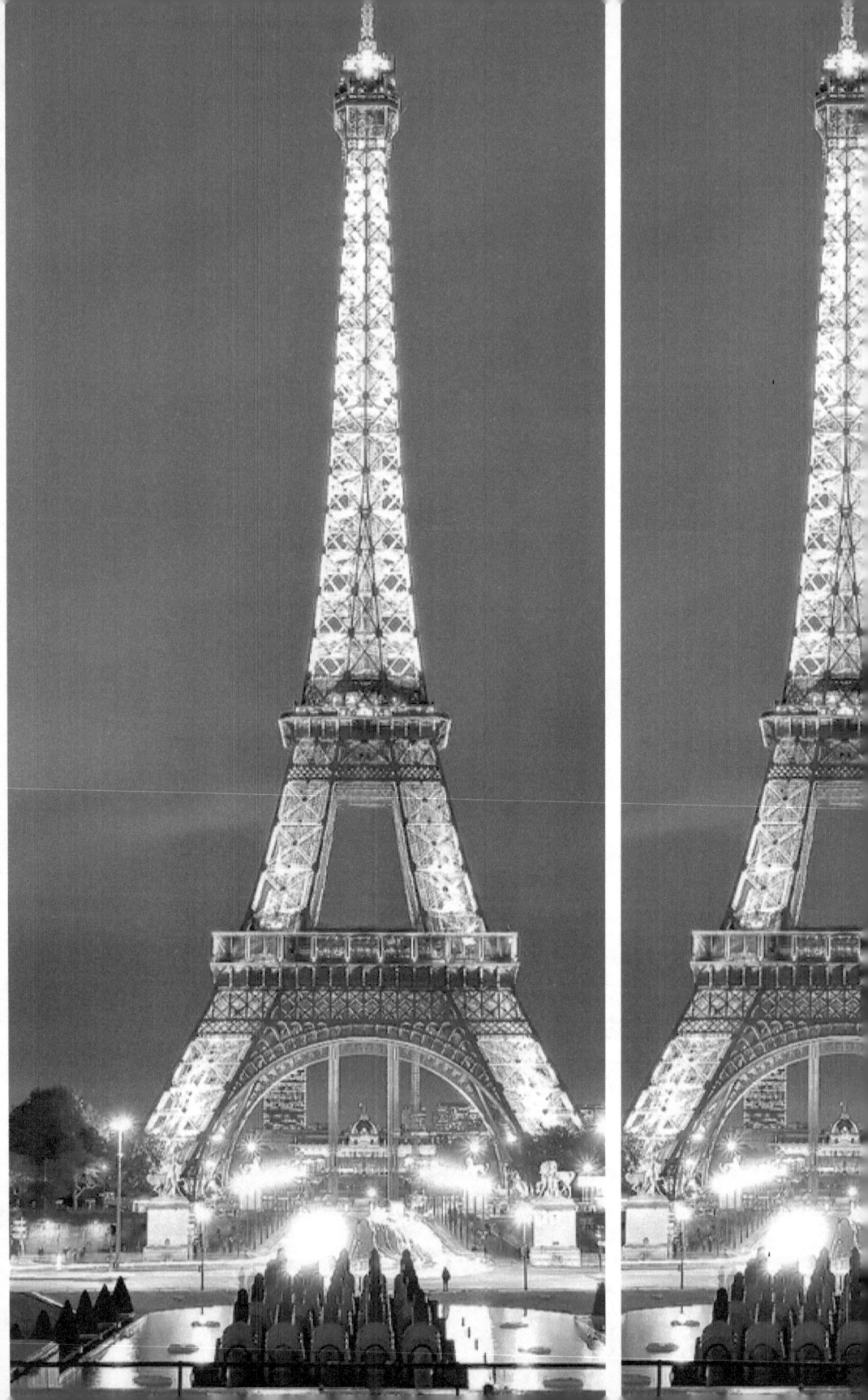

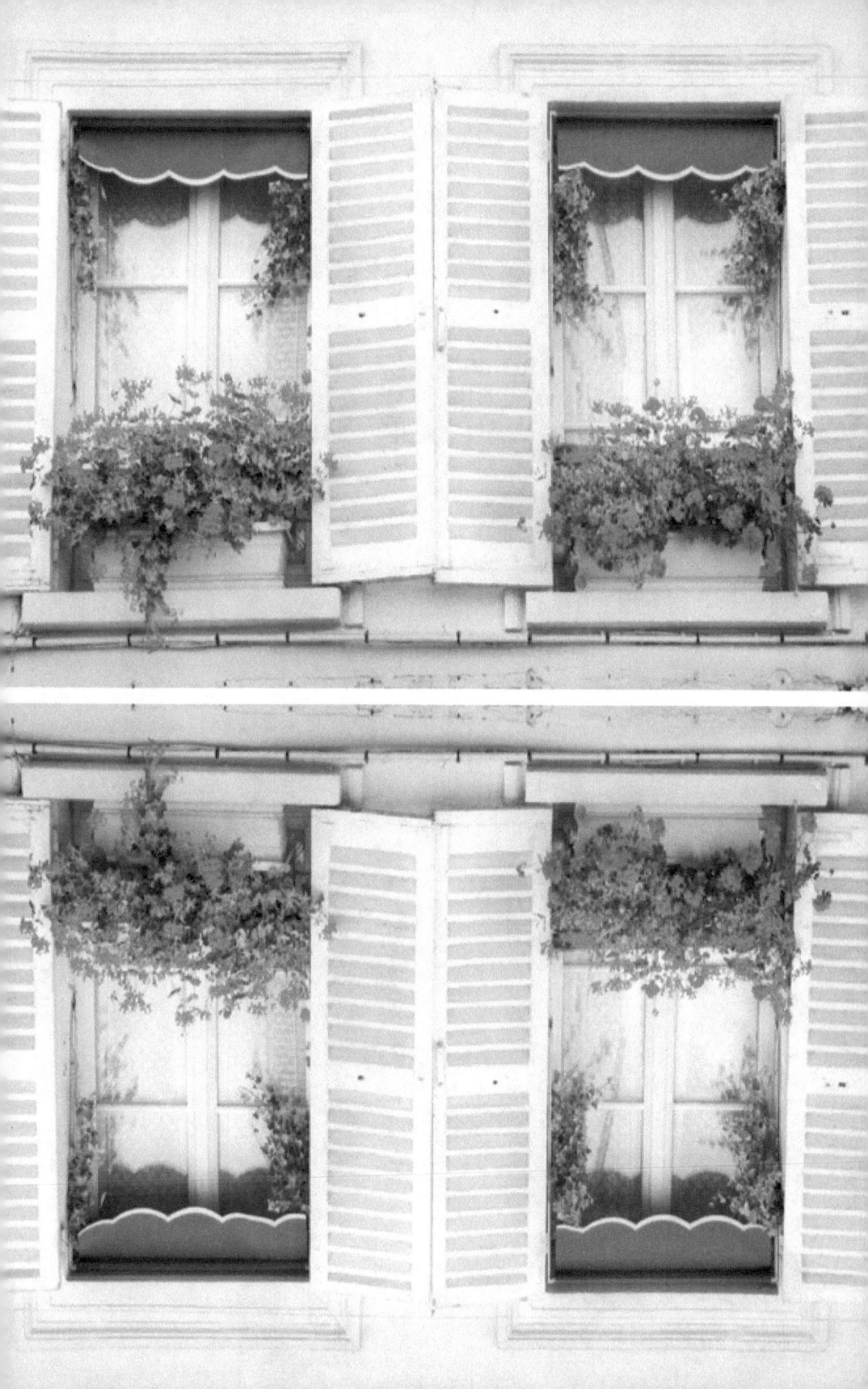

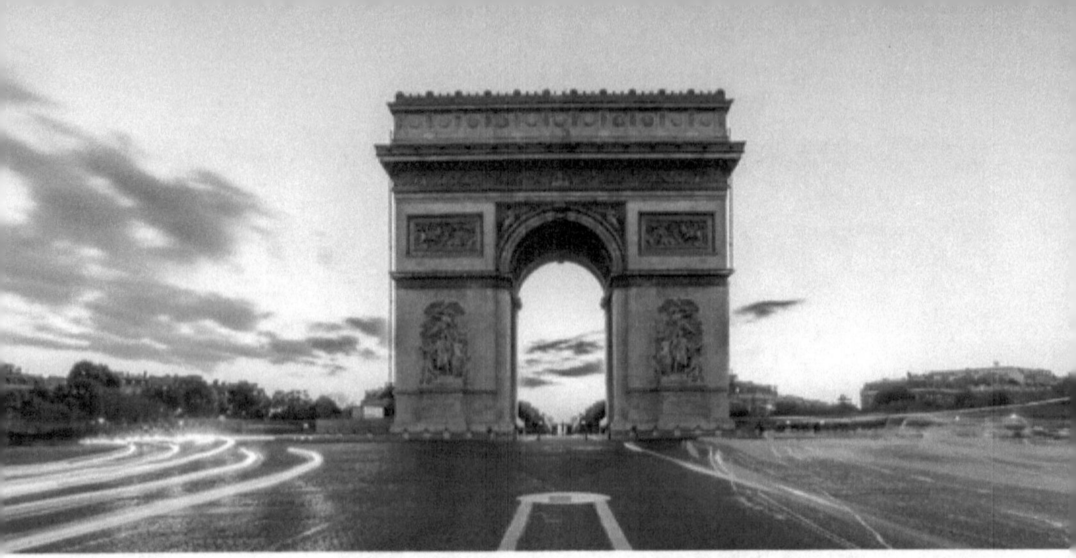

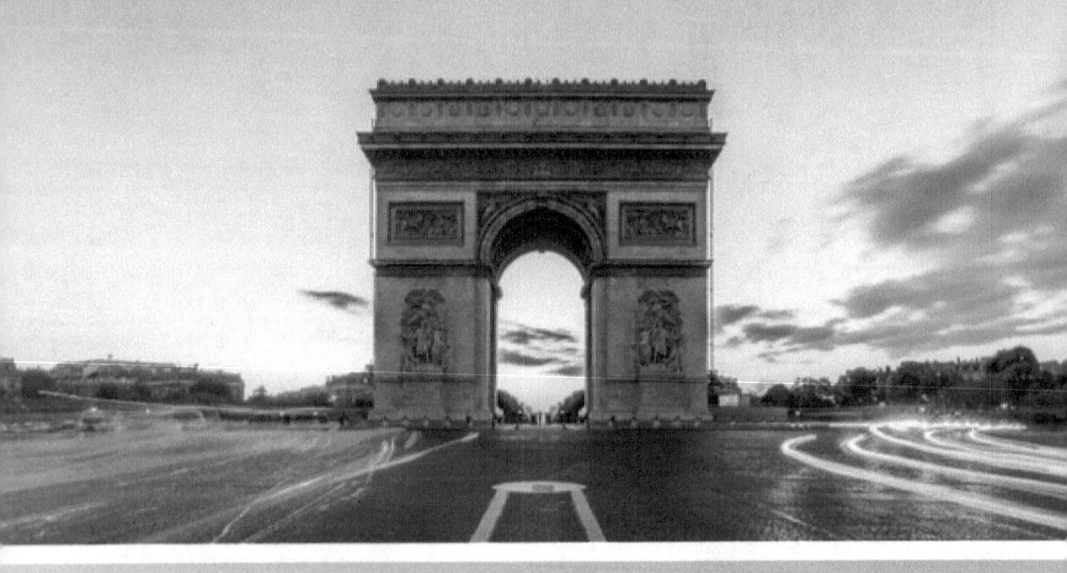
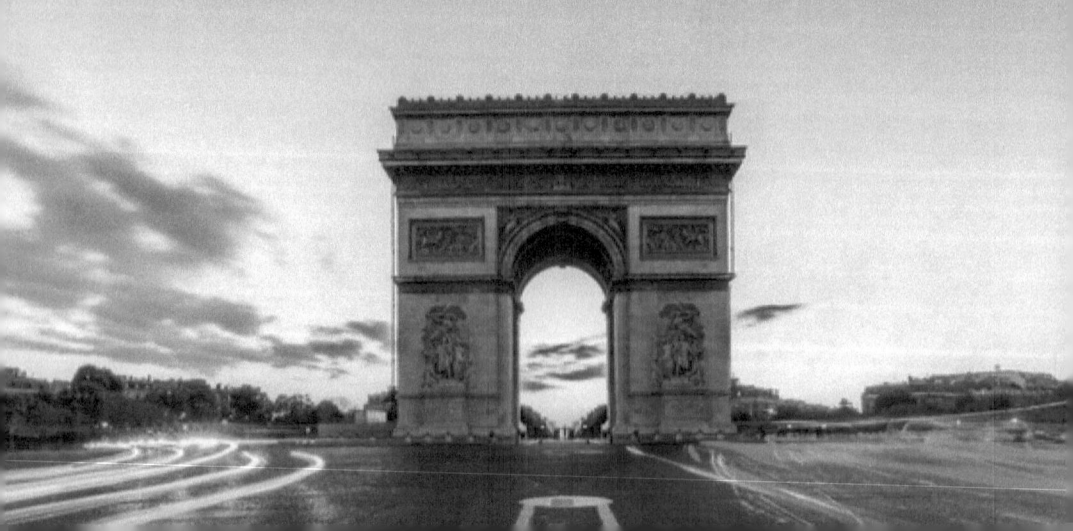

"When good Americans die, they go to Paris."
Oscar Wilde

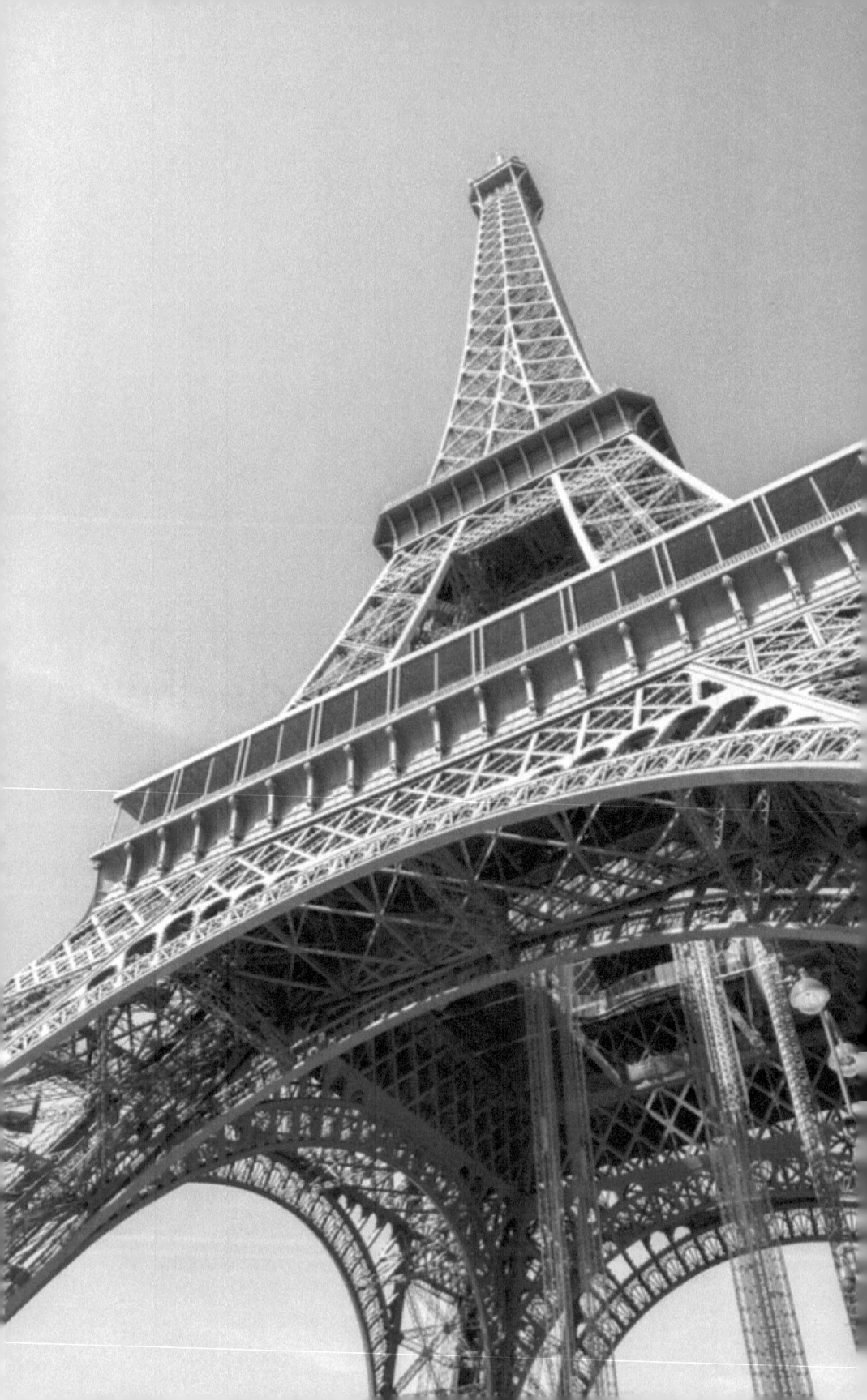

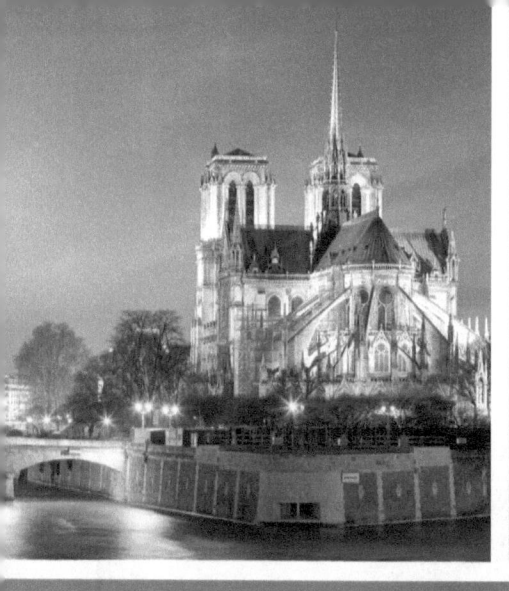
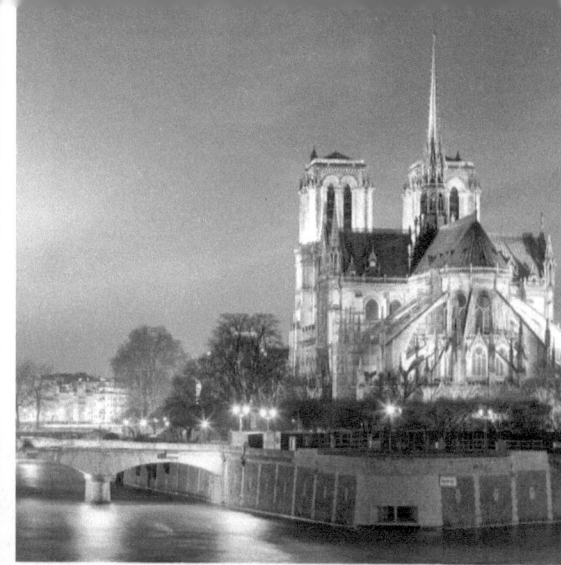

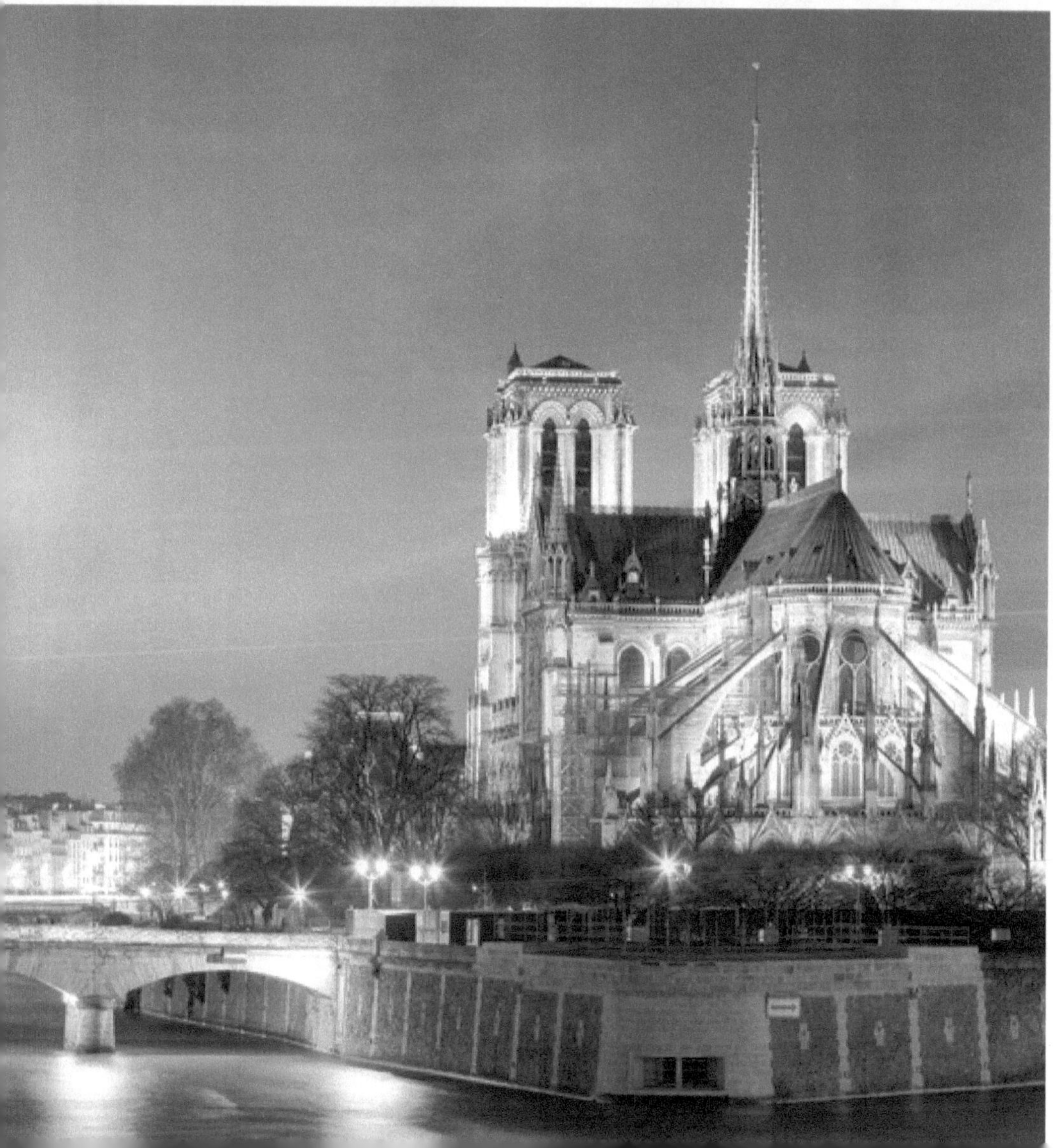

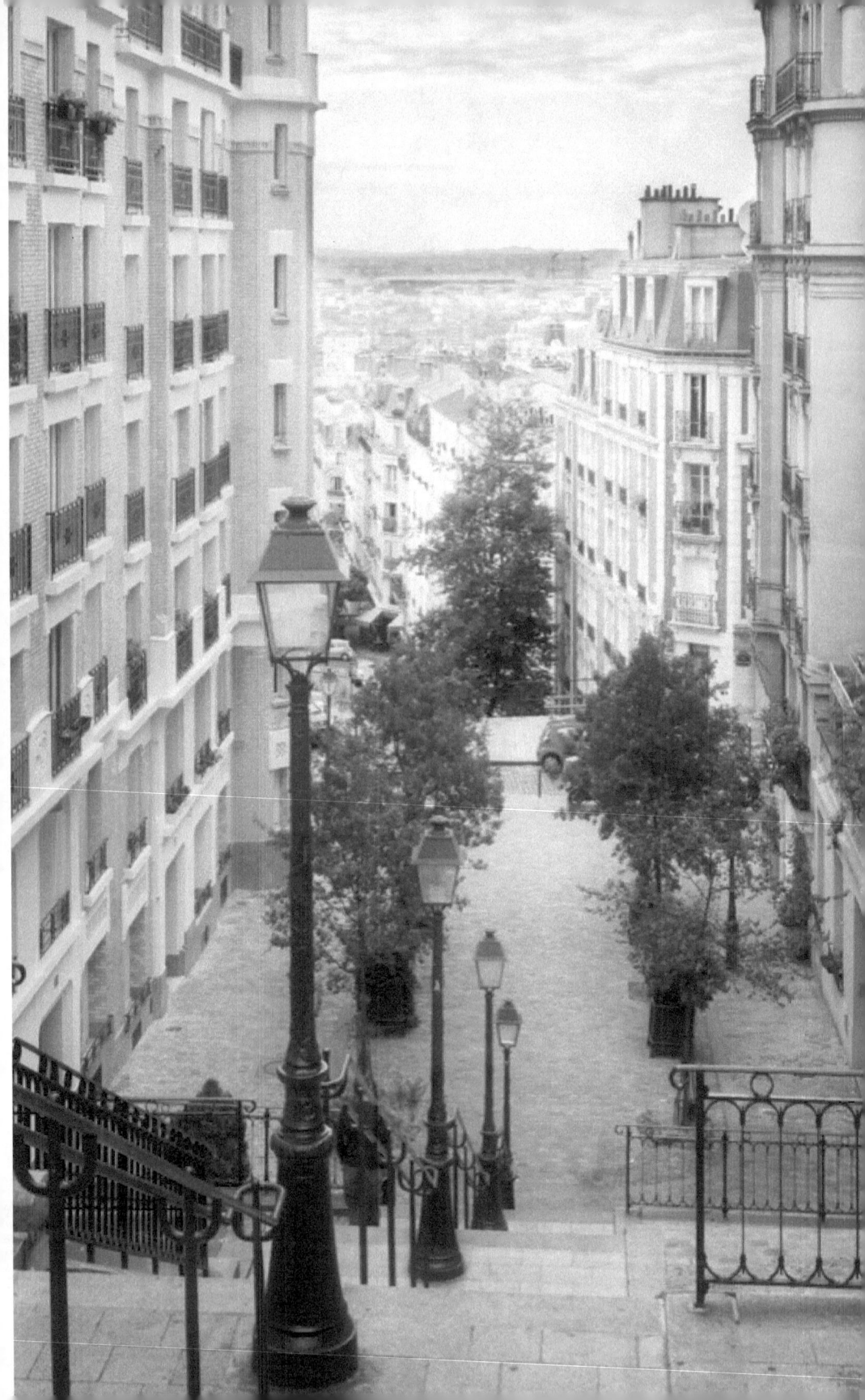

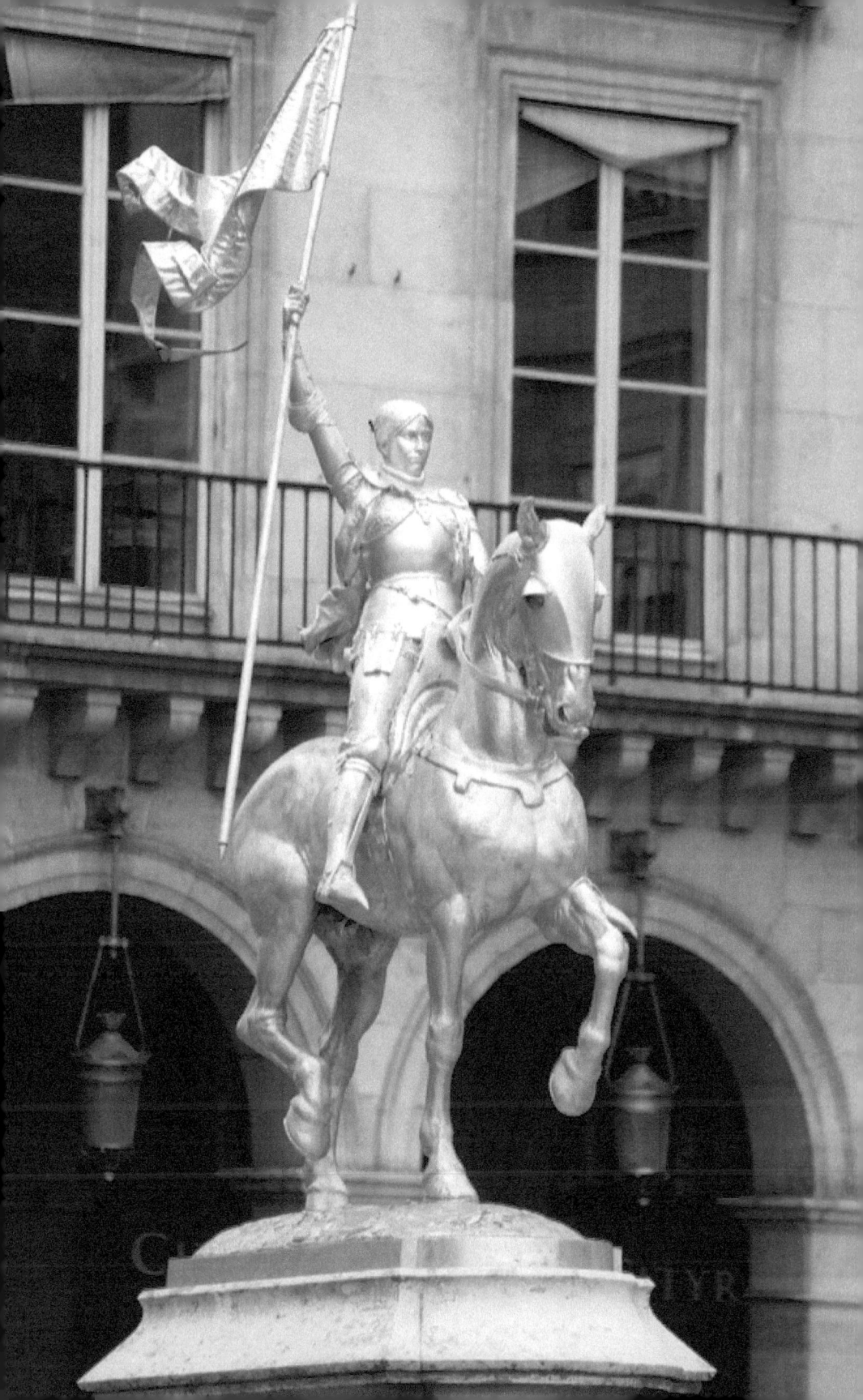

"To know Paris is to know a great deal." – Henry Miller

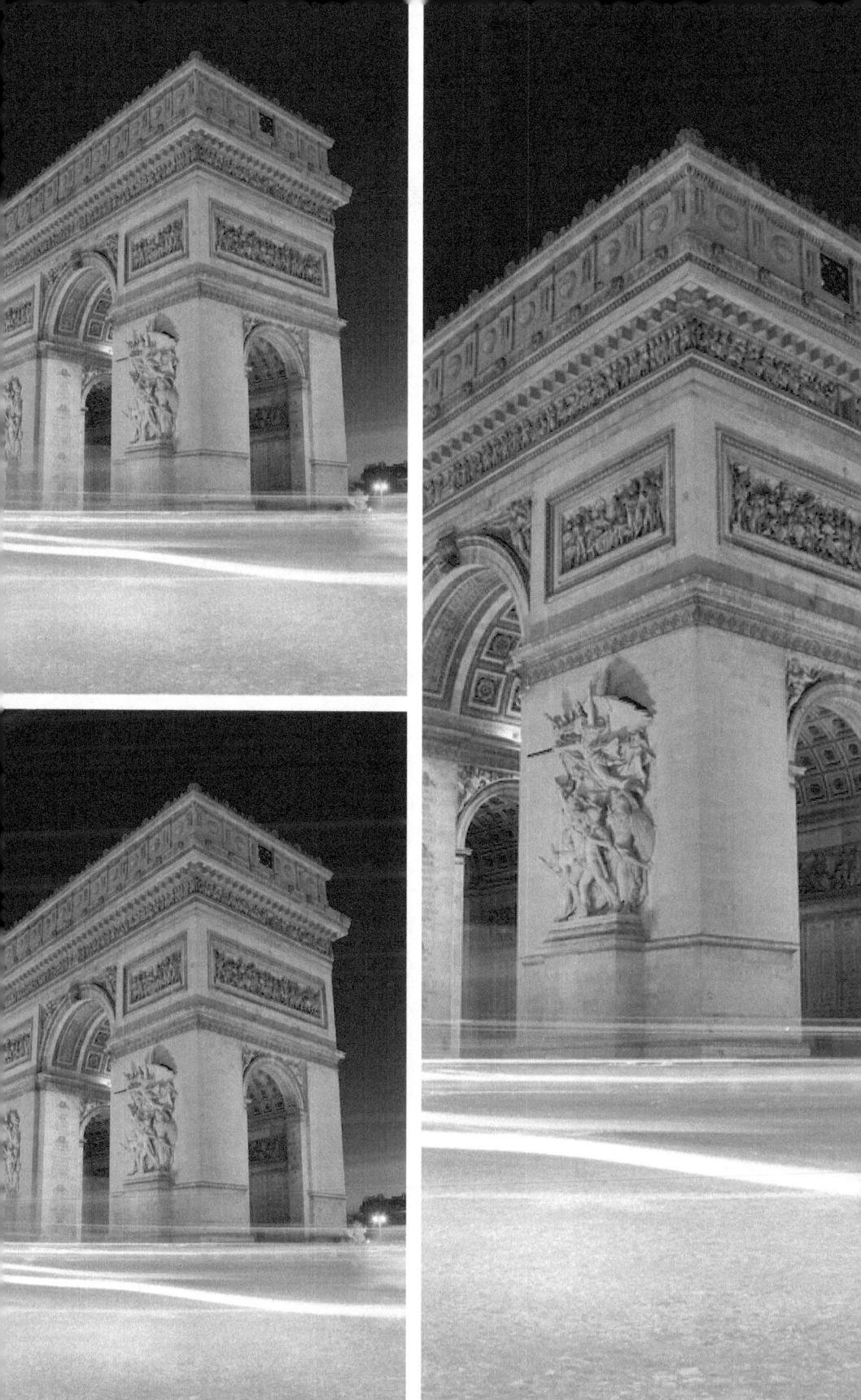

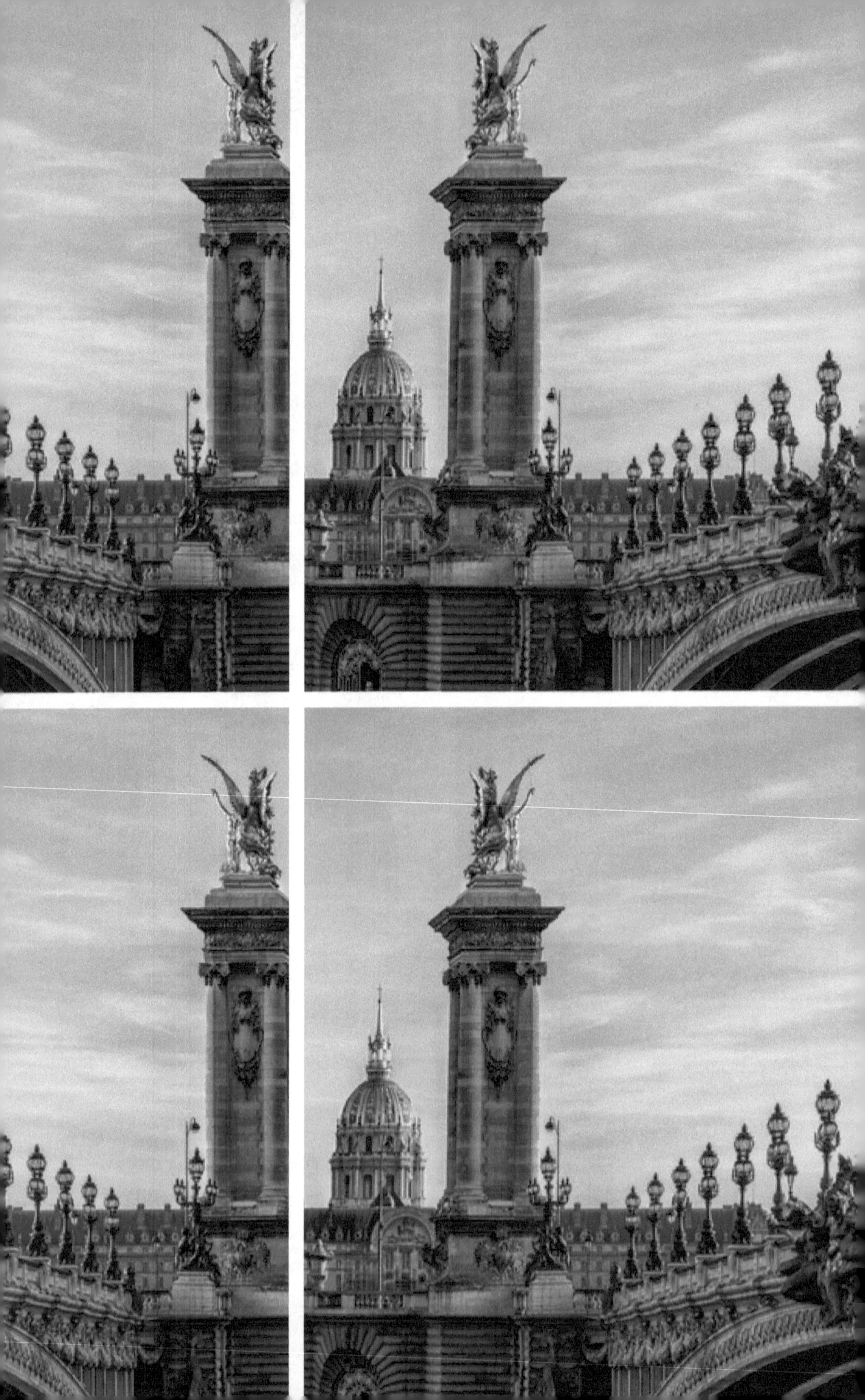

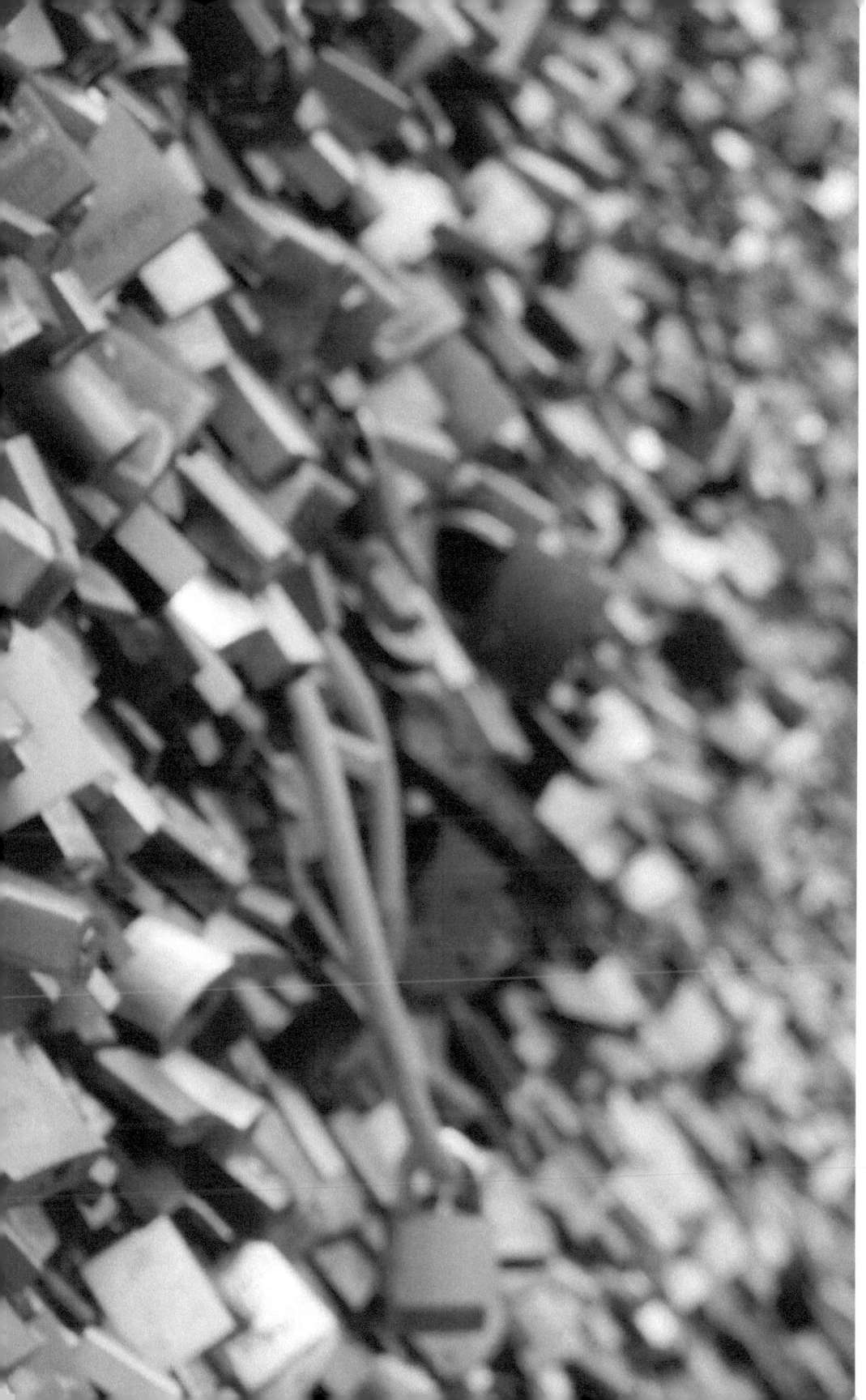

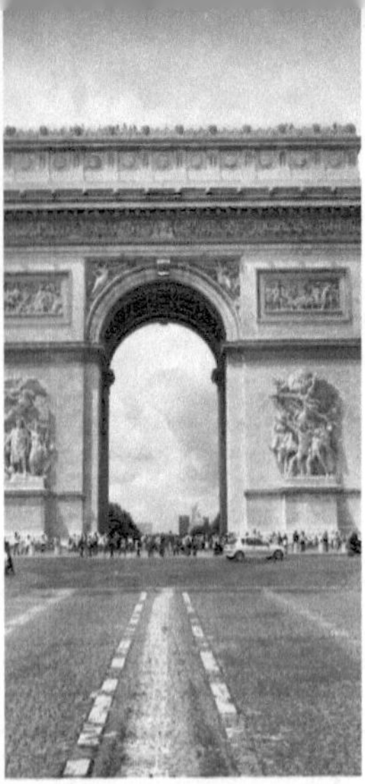

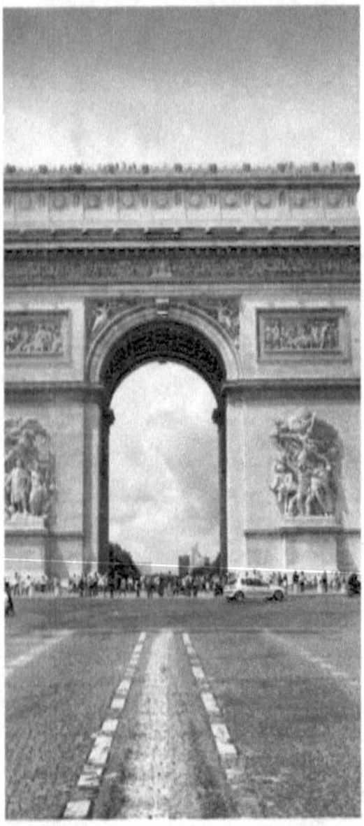

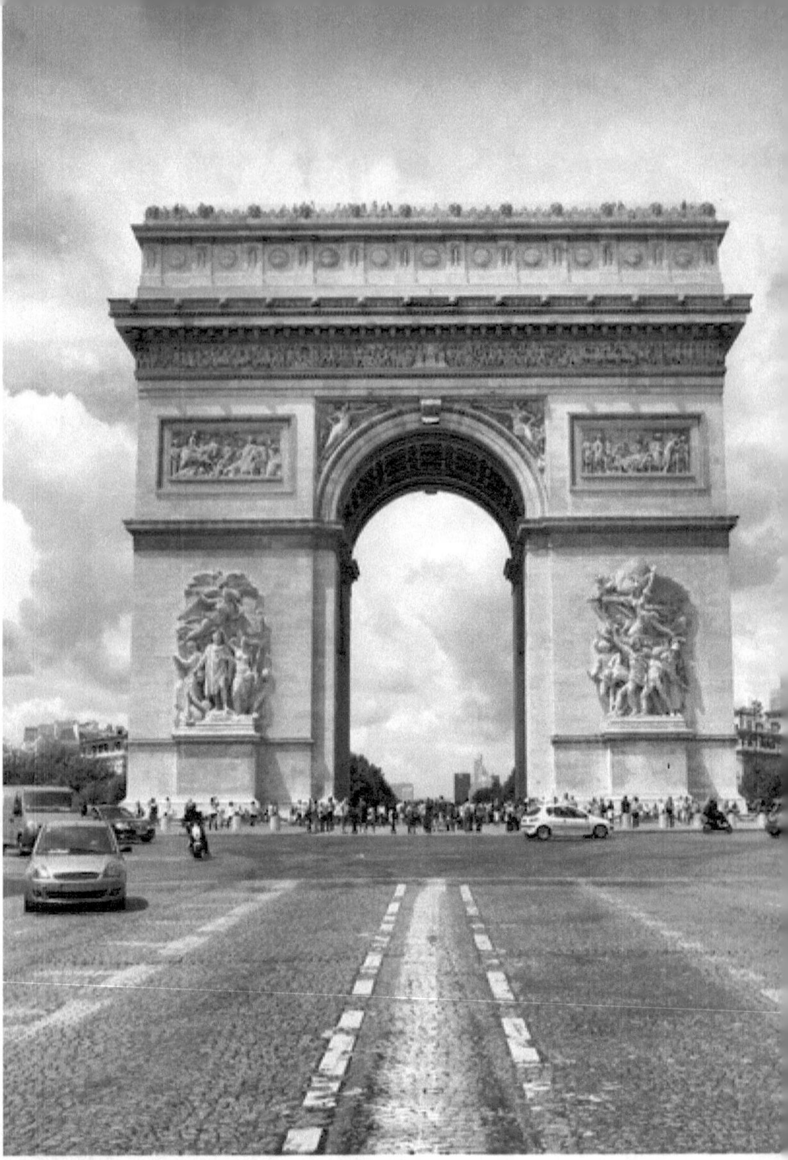

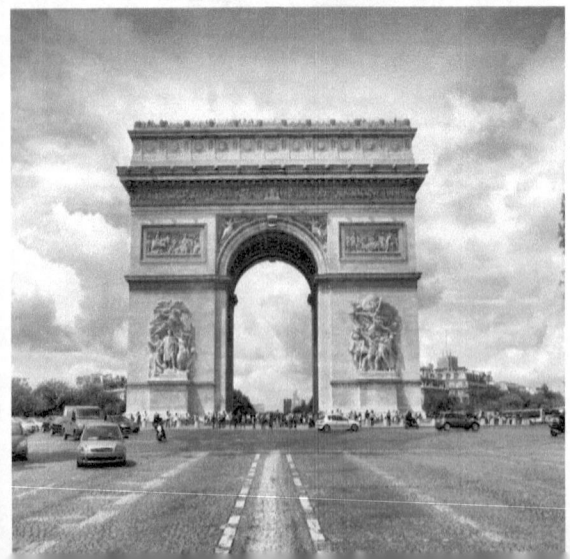
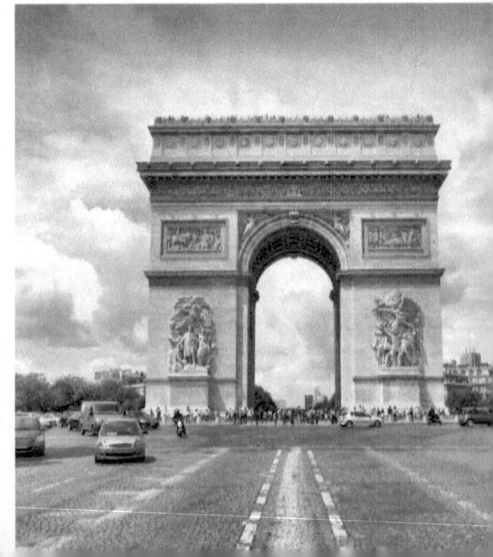

"You know, I sometimes think, how is anyone ever gonna come up with a book, or a painting, or a symphony, or a sculpture that can compete with a great city. You can't. Because you look around and every street, every boulevard, is its own special art form and when you think that in the cold, violent, meaningless universe that Paris exists, these lights. I mean come on, there's nothing happening on Jupiter or Neptune, but from way out in space you can see these lights, the cafés, people drinking and singing. For all we know, Paris is the hottest spot in the universe." – Owen Wilson

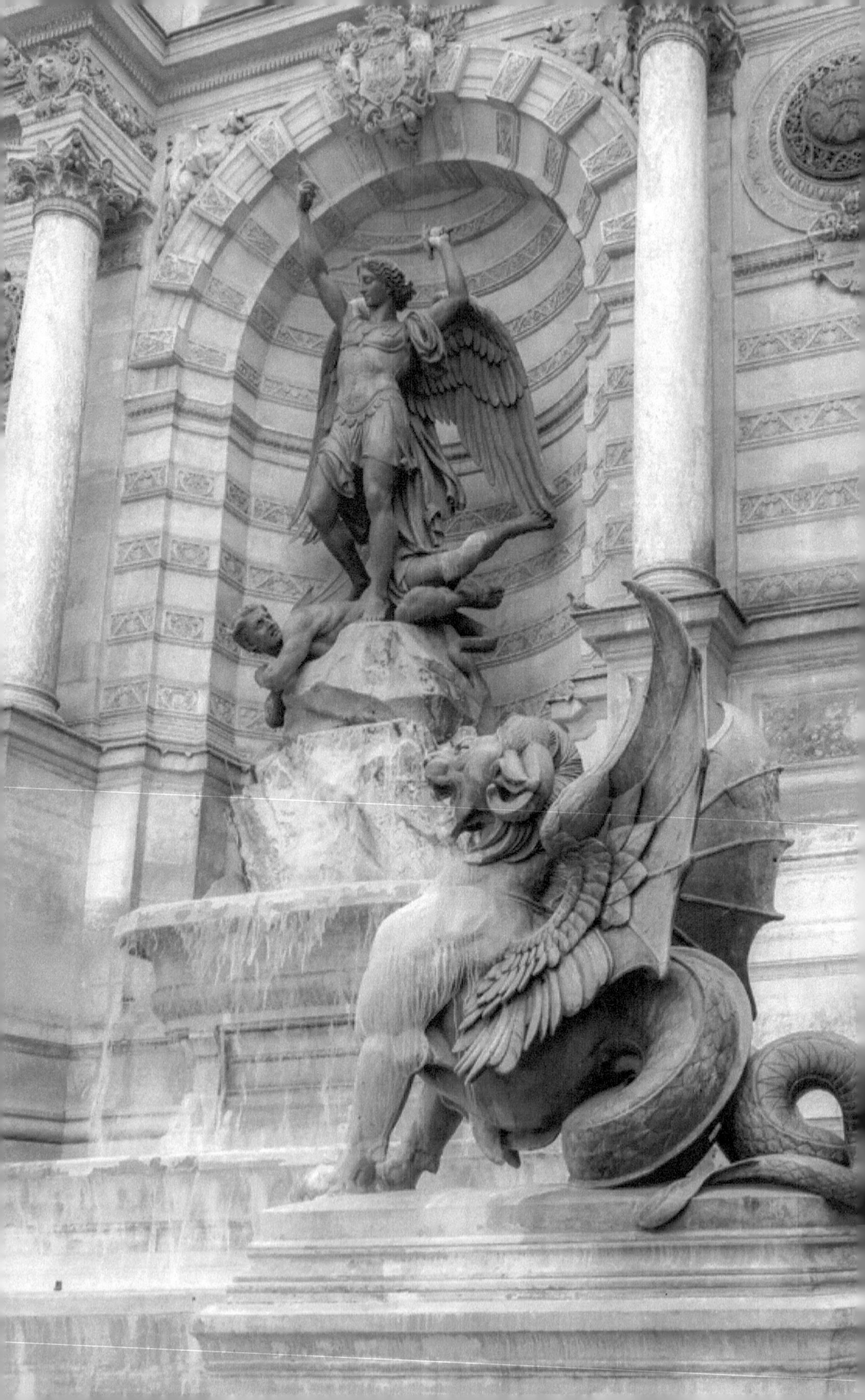

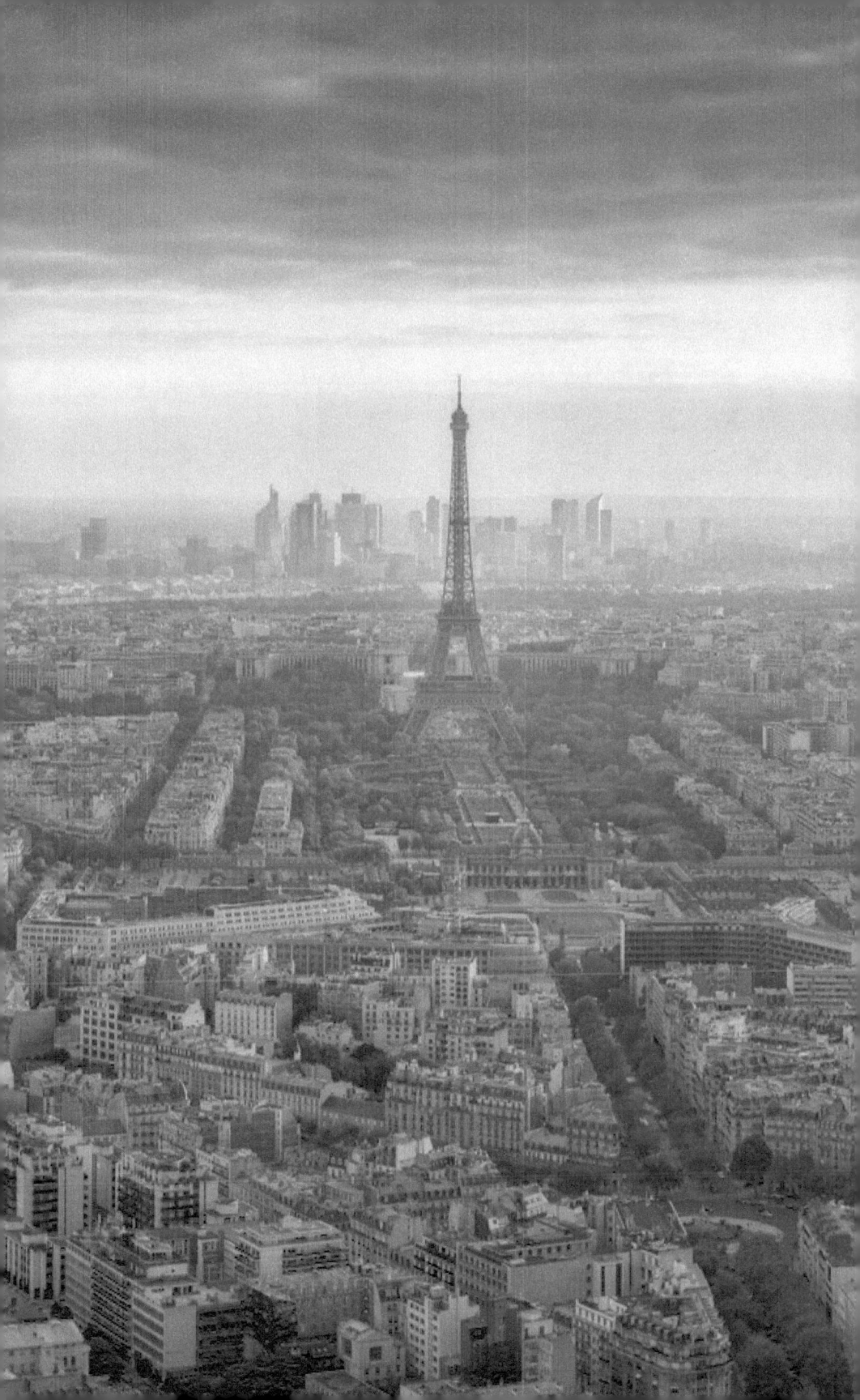

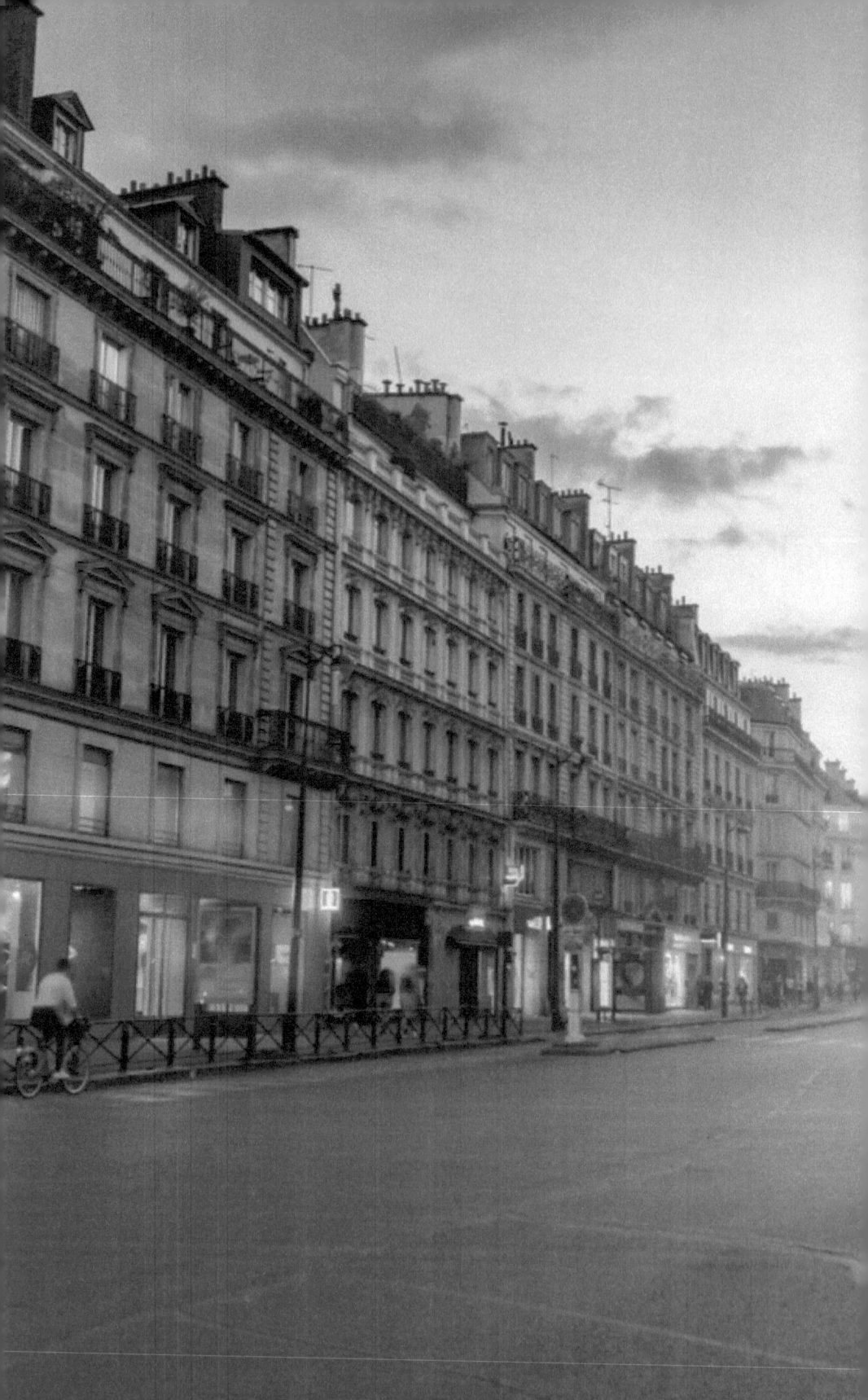

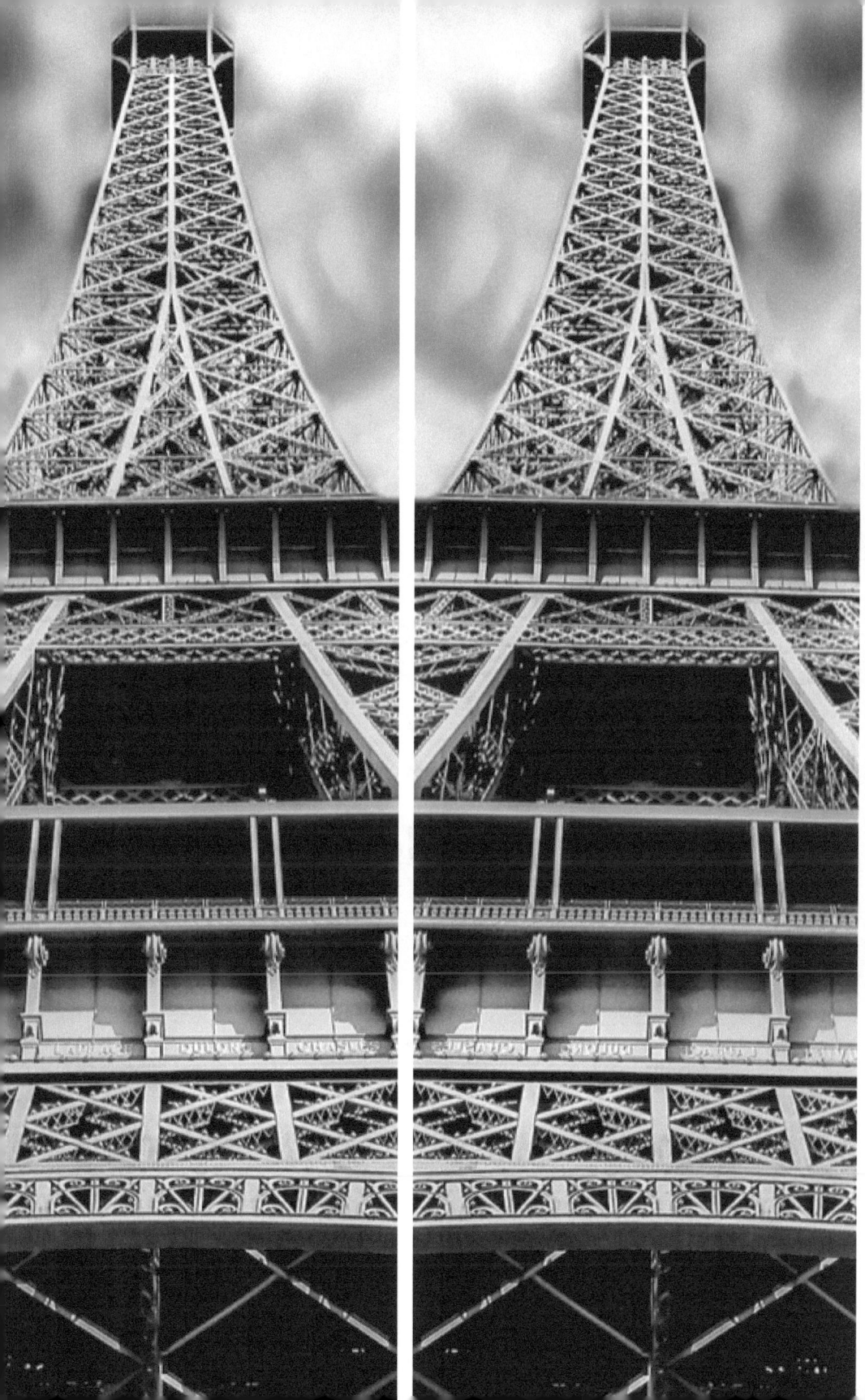

A walk about Paris will provide lessons in history, beauty, and in the point of Life."
Thomas Jefferson.

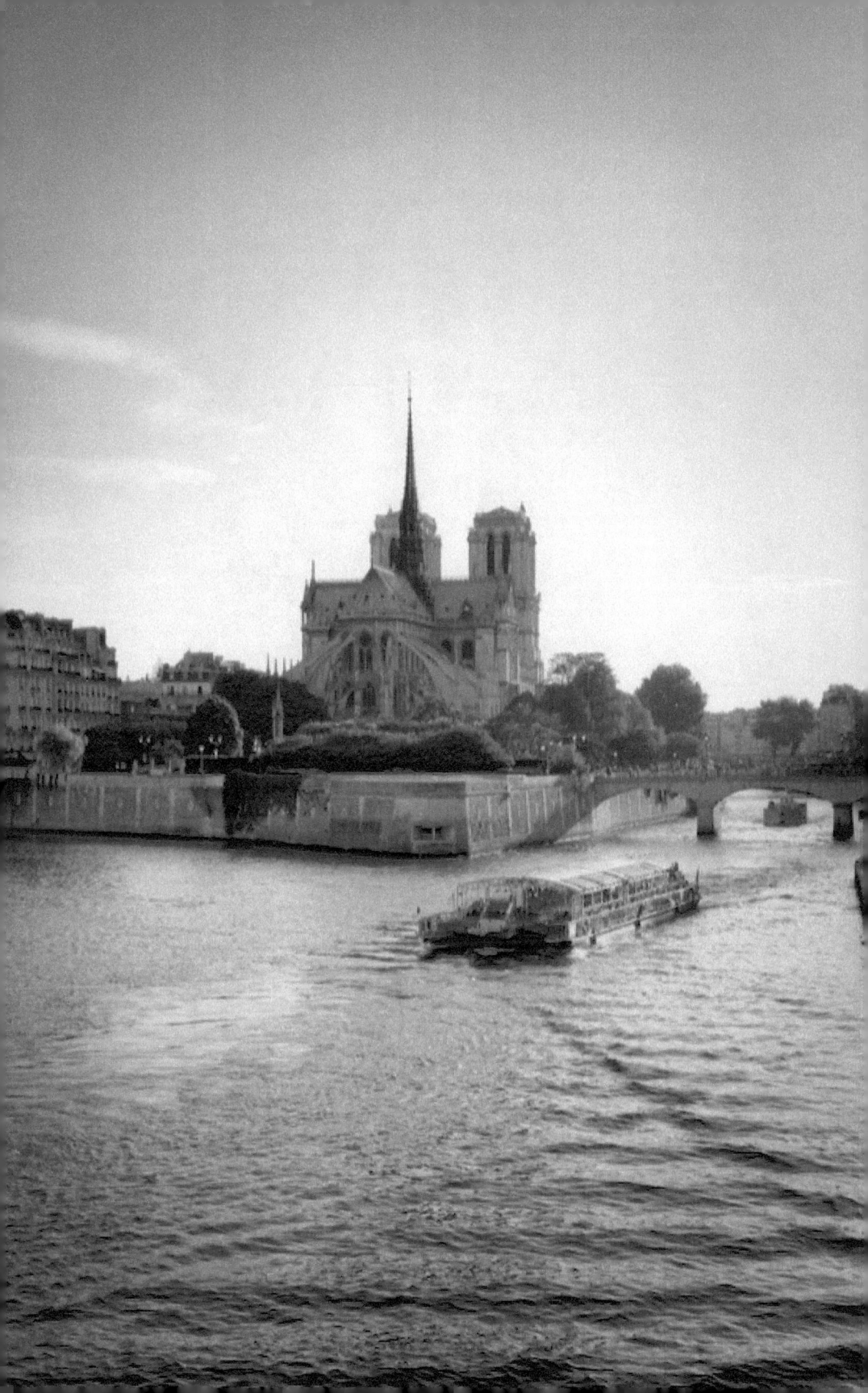

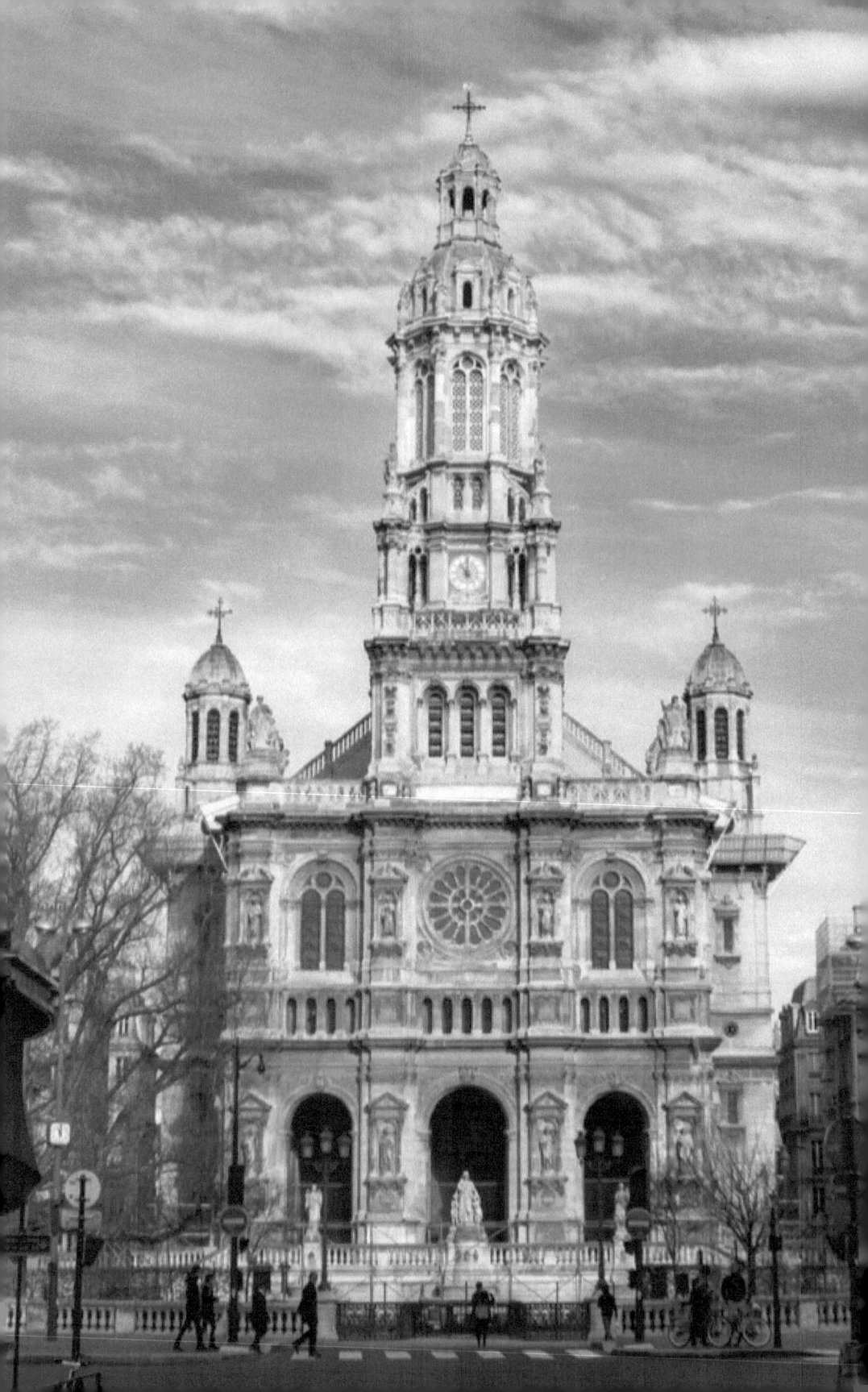

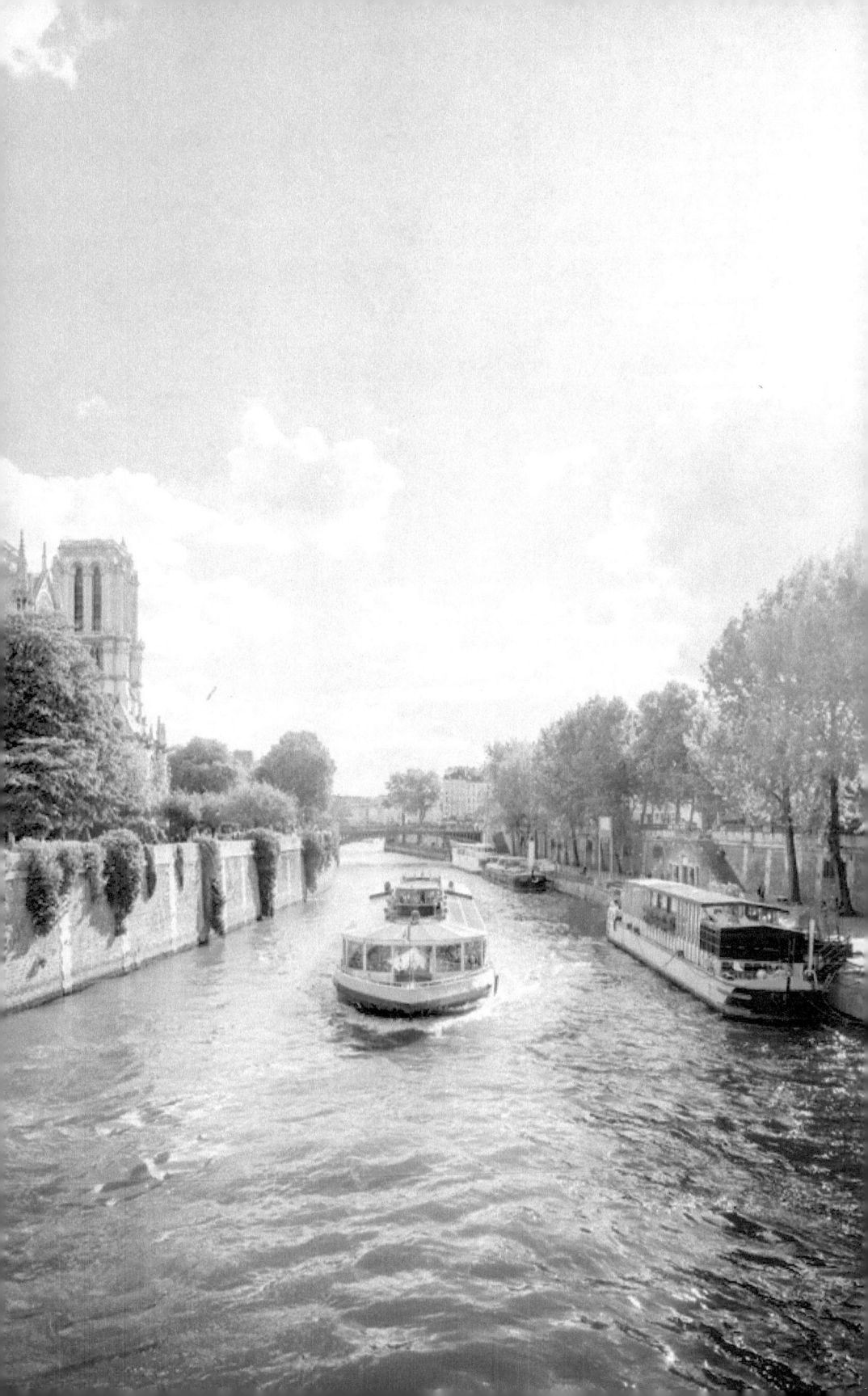

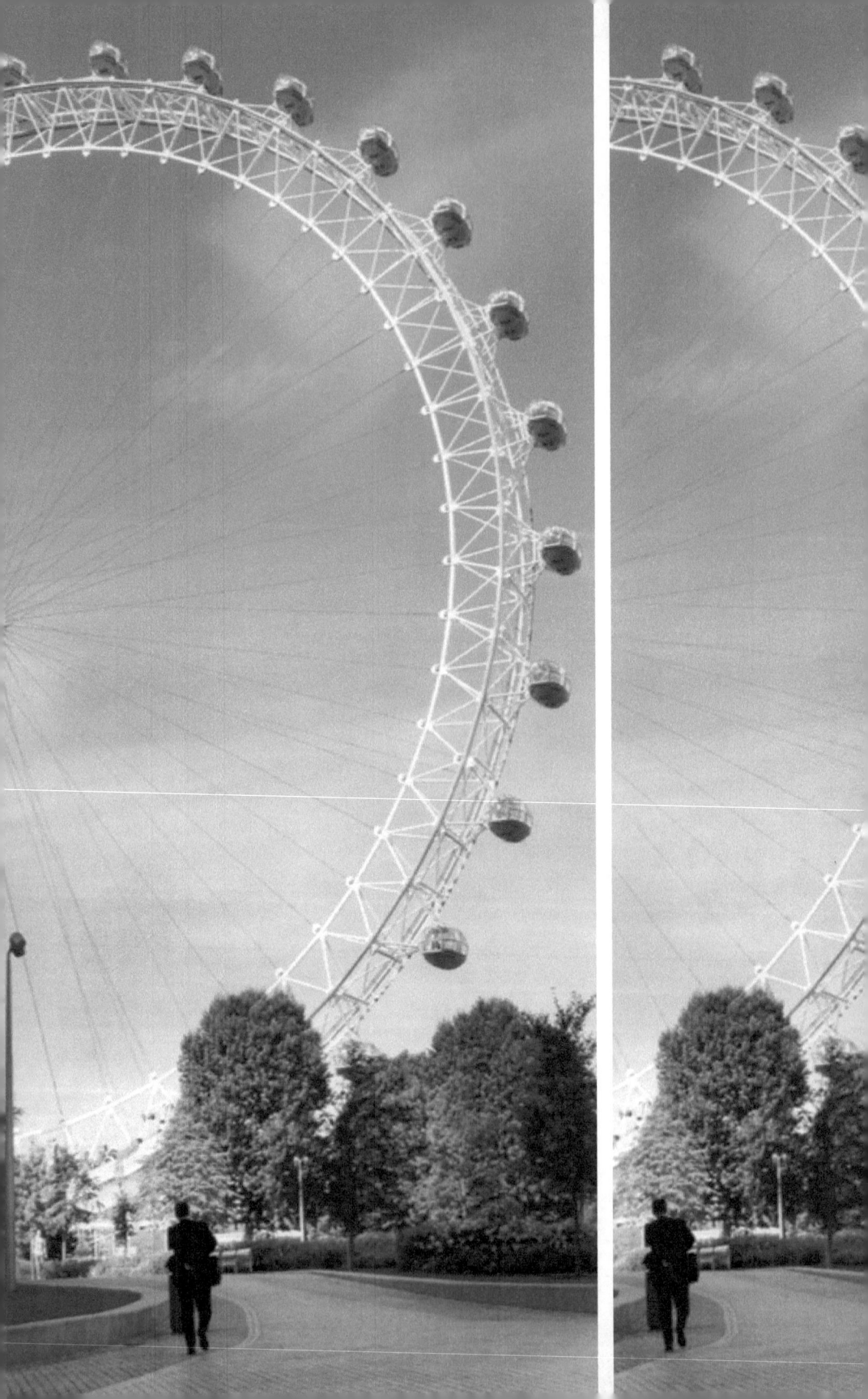

"Paris was a universe whole and entire unto herself, hollowed and fashioned by history; so she seemed in this age of Napoleon III with her towering buildings, her massive cathedrals, her grand boulevards and ancient winding medieval streets-as vast and indestructible as nature itself.

All was embraced by her, by her volatile and enchanted populace thronging the galleries, the theaters, the cafes, giving birth over and over to genius and sanctity, philosophy and war, frivolity and the finest art; so it seemed that if all the world outside her were to sink into darkness, what was fine, what was beautiful, what was essential might there still come to its finest flower. Even the majestic trees that graced and sheltered her streets were attuned to her-and the waters of the Seine, contained and beautiful as they wound through her heart; so that the earth on that spot, so shaped by blood and consciousness, had ceased to be the earth and had become Paris."

Anne Rice.

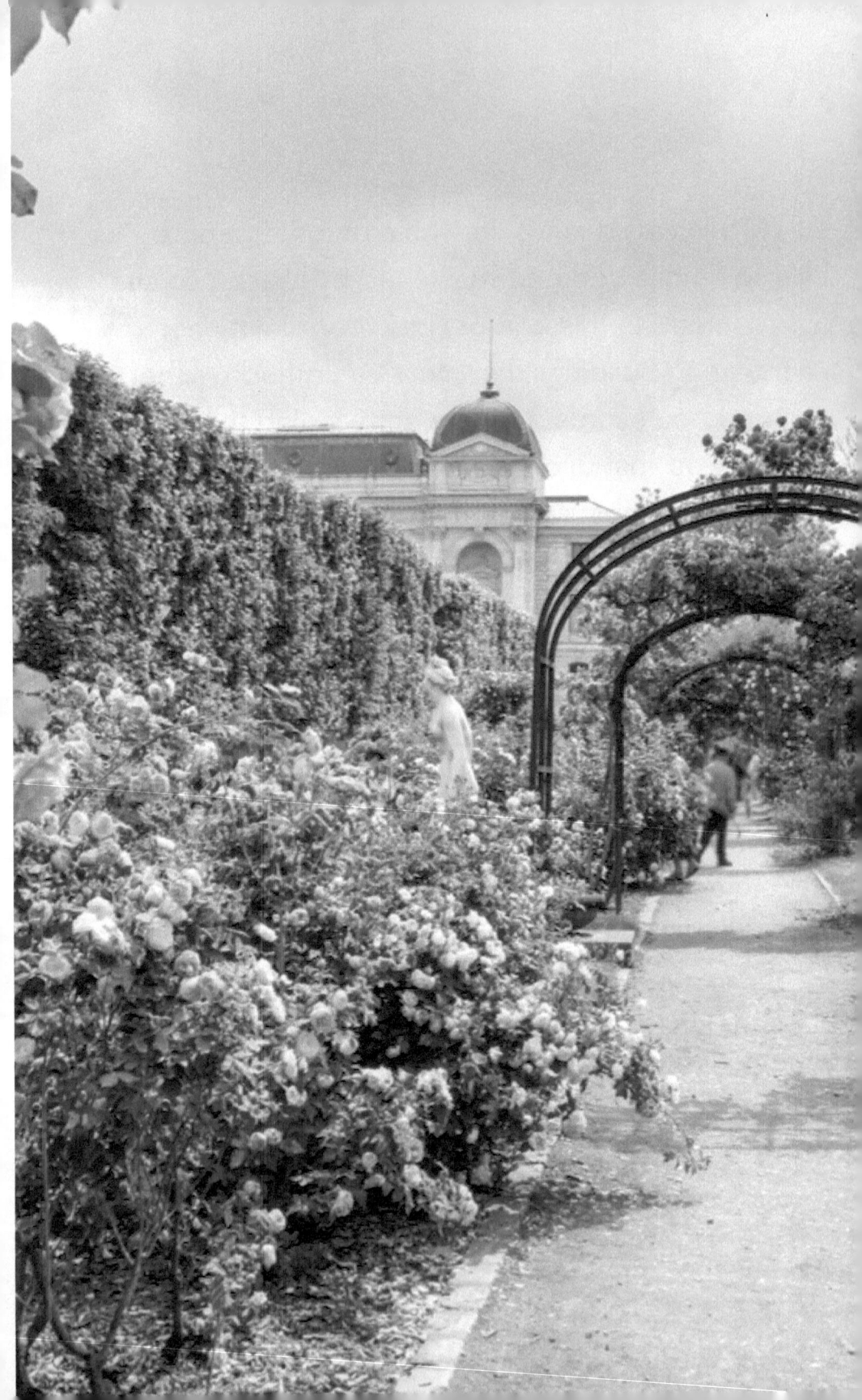

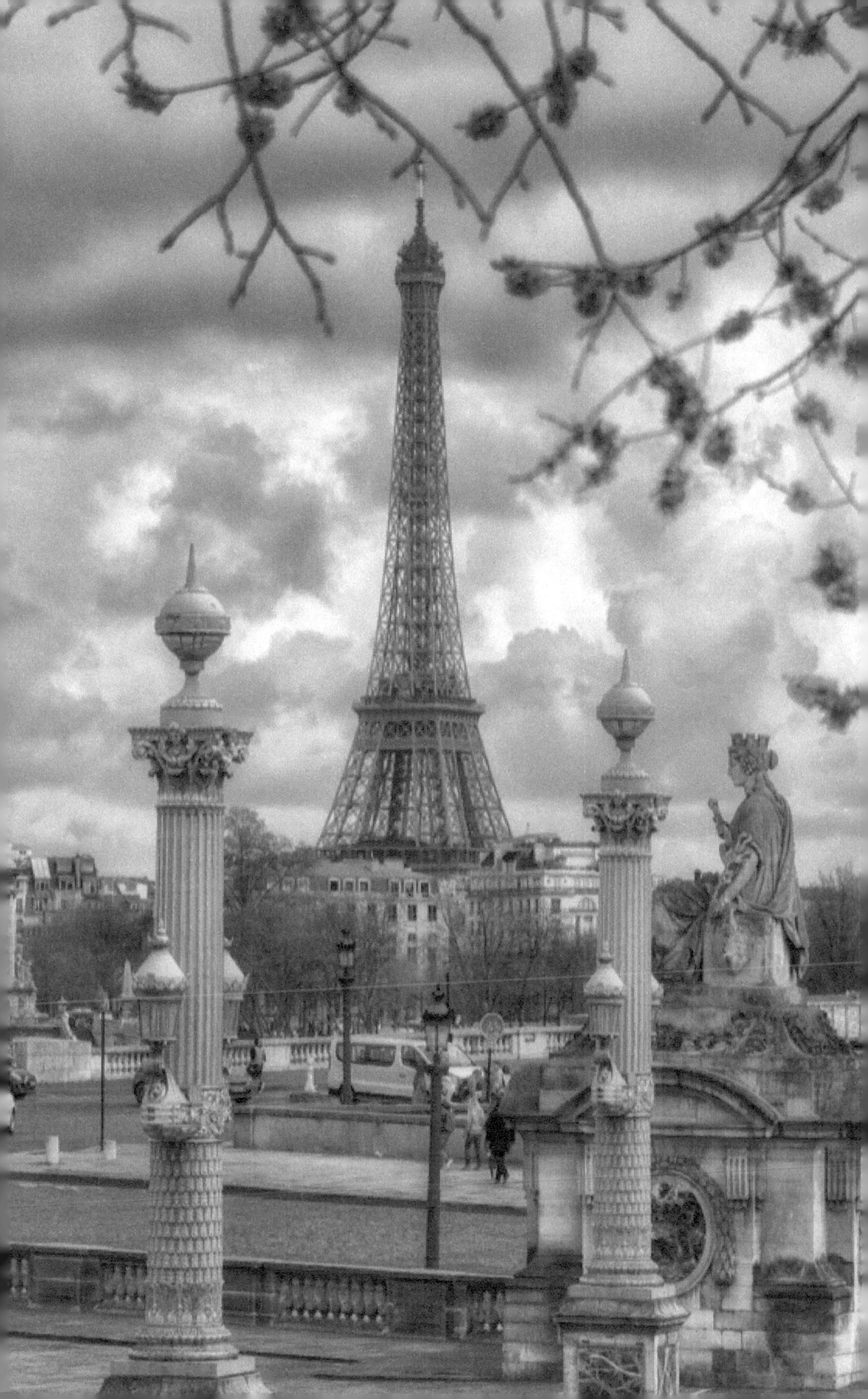

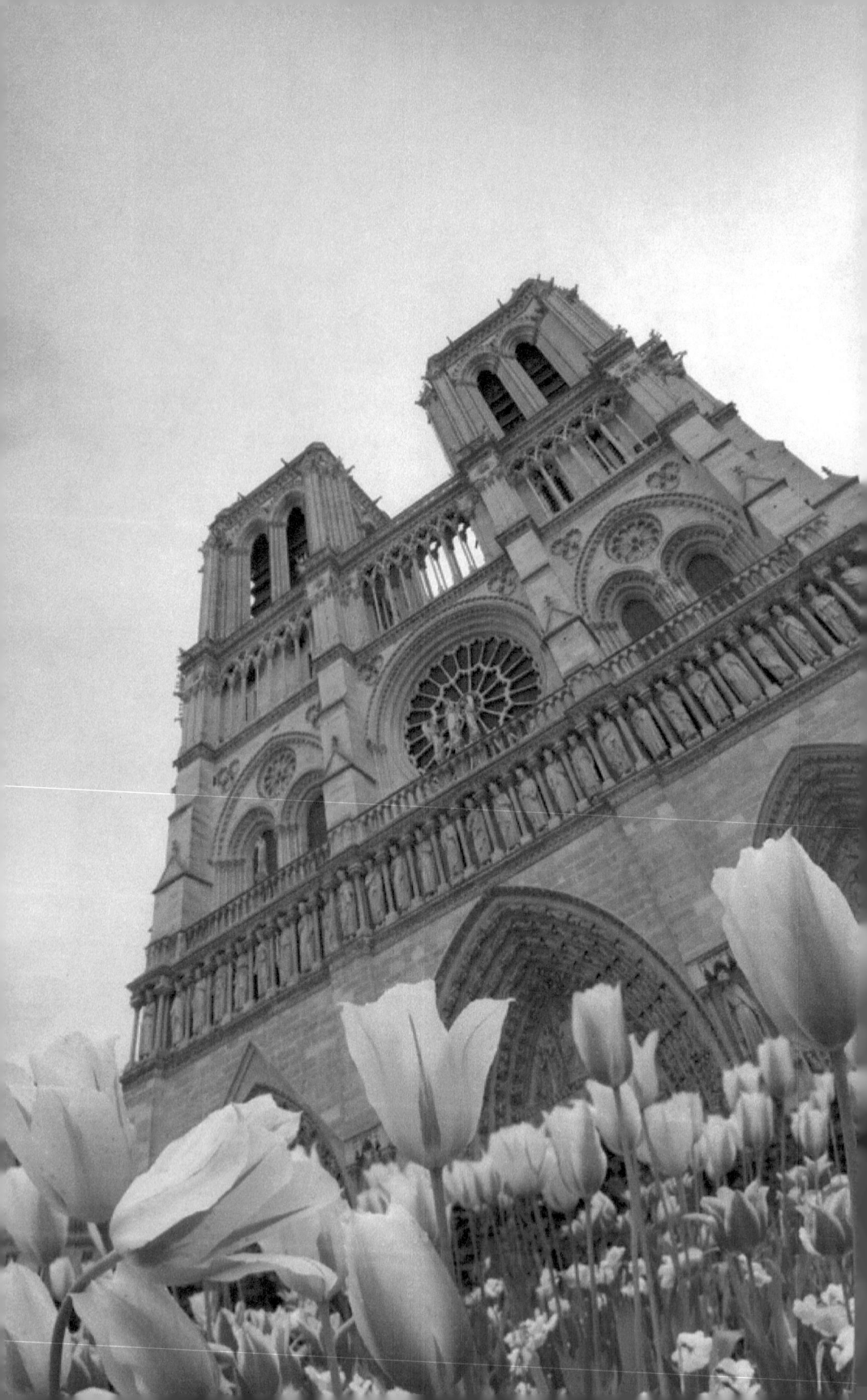

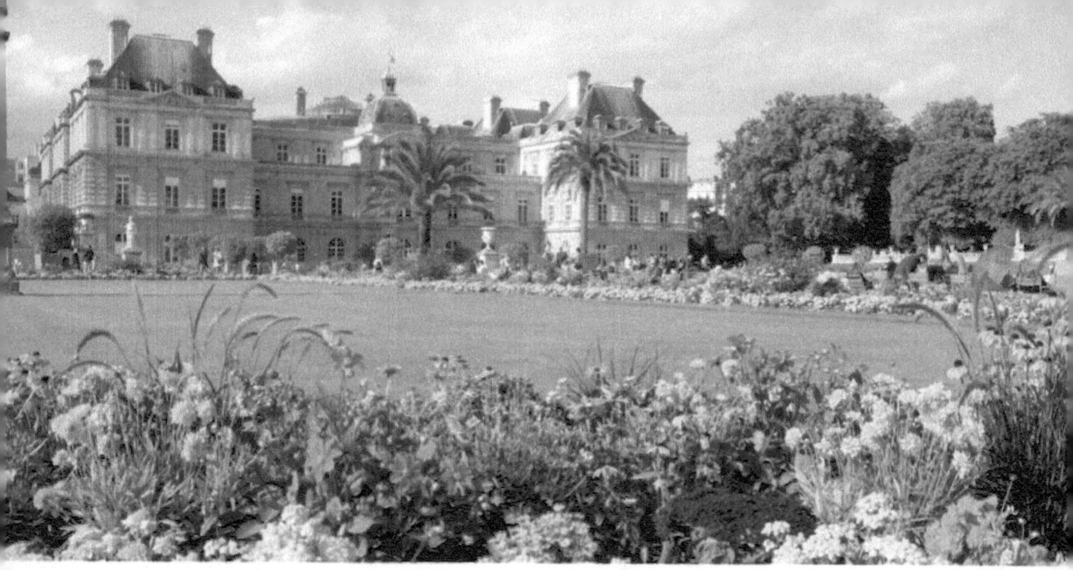

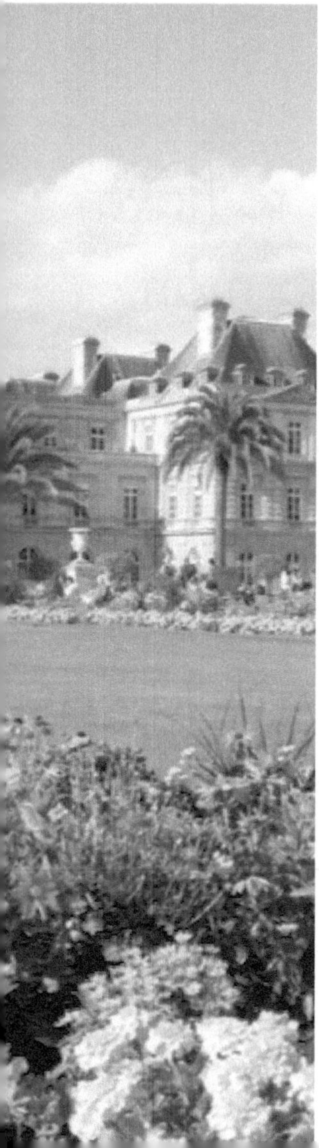

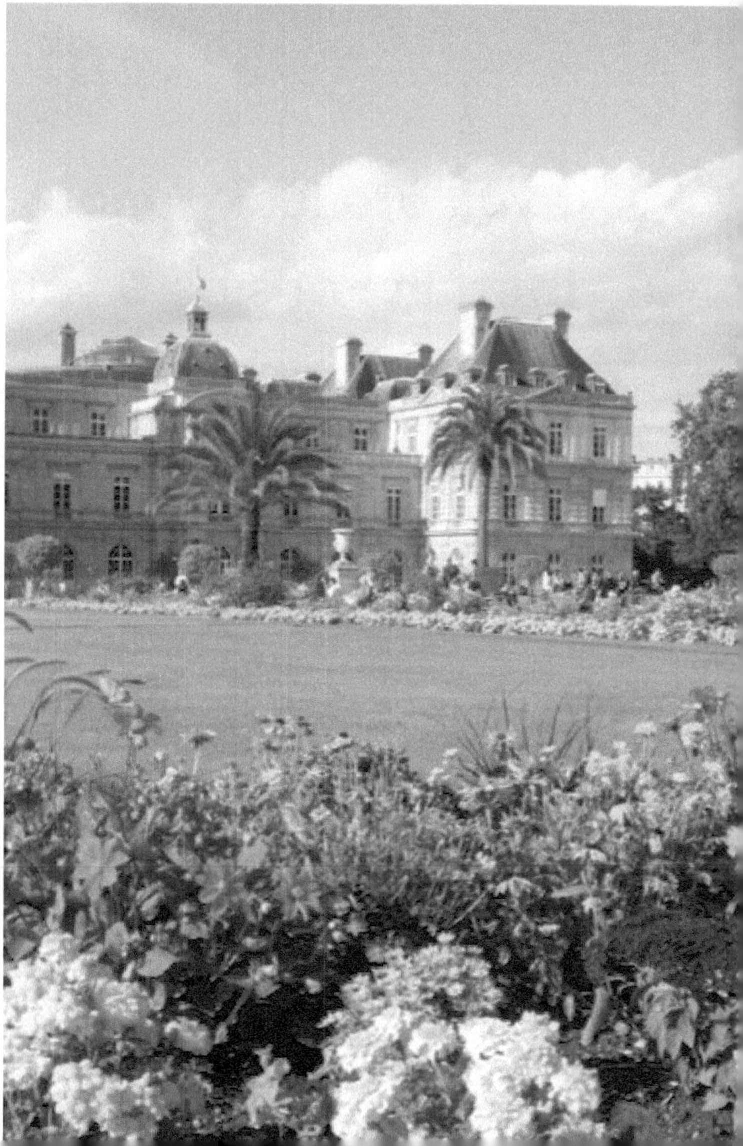

"If you are lucky enough to have lived in Paris as a young man, then wherever you go for the rest of your life it stays with you, for Paris is a moveable feast." – Ernest Hemingway

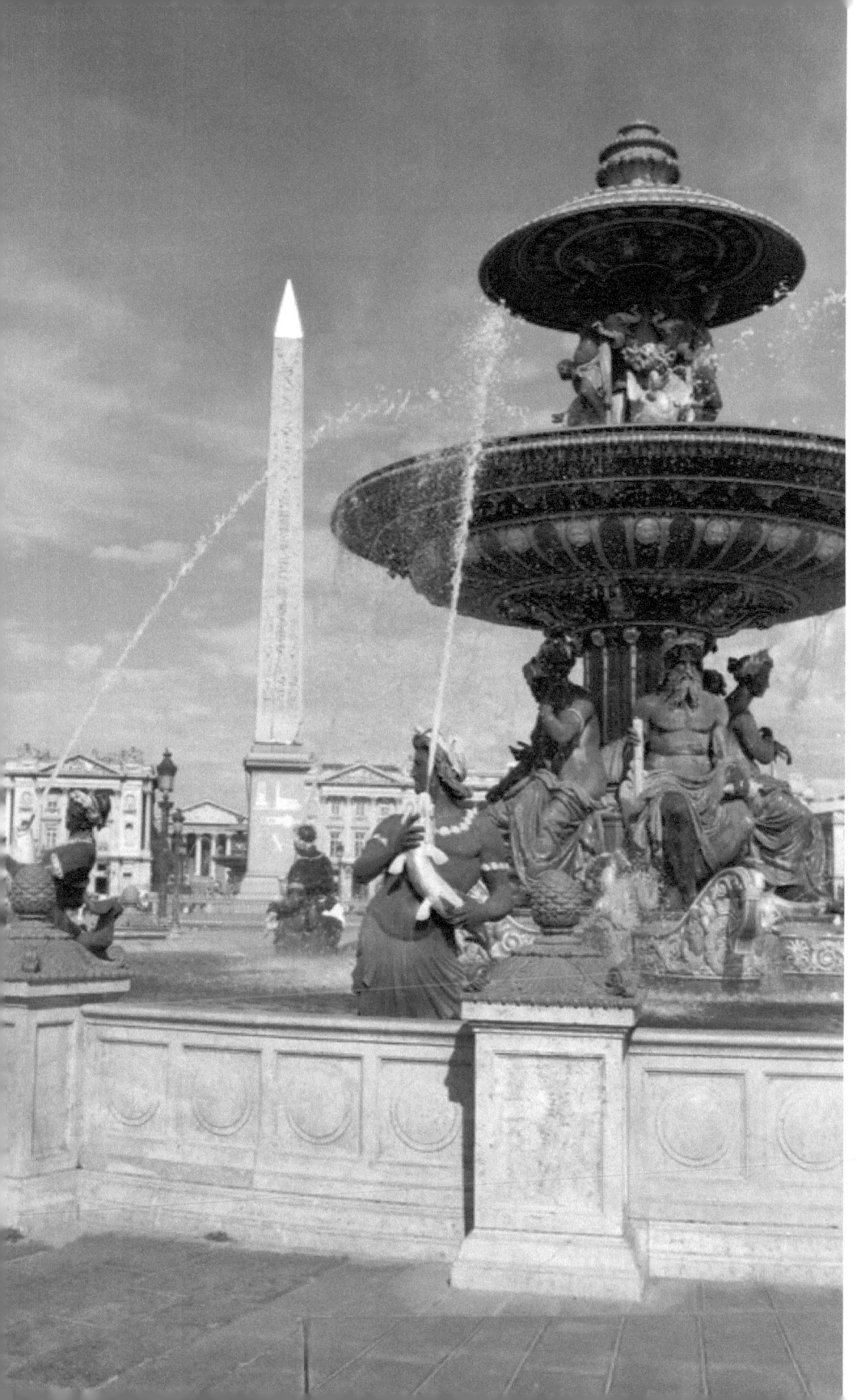

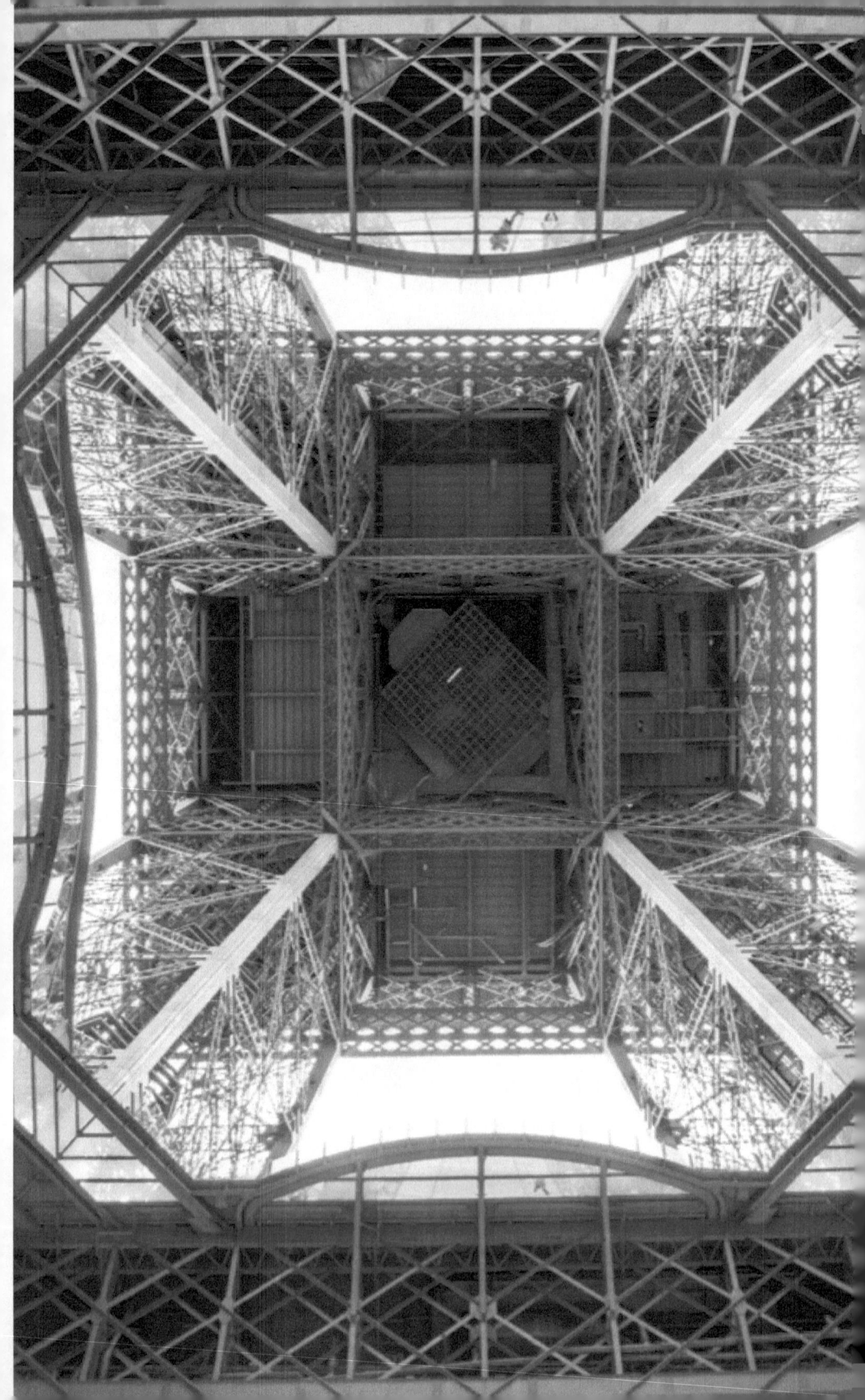

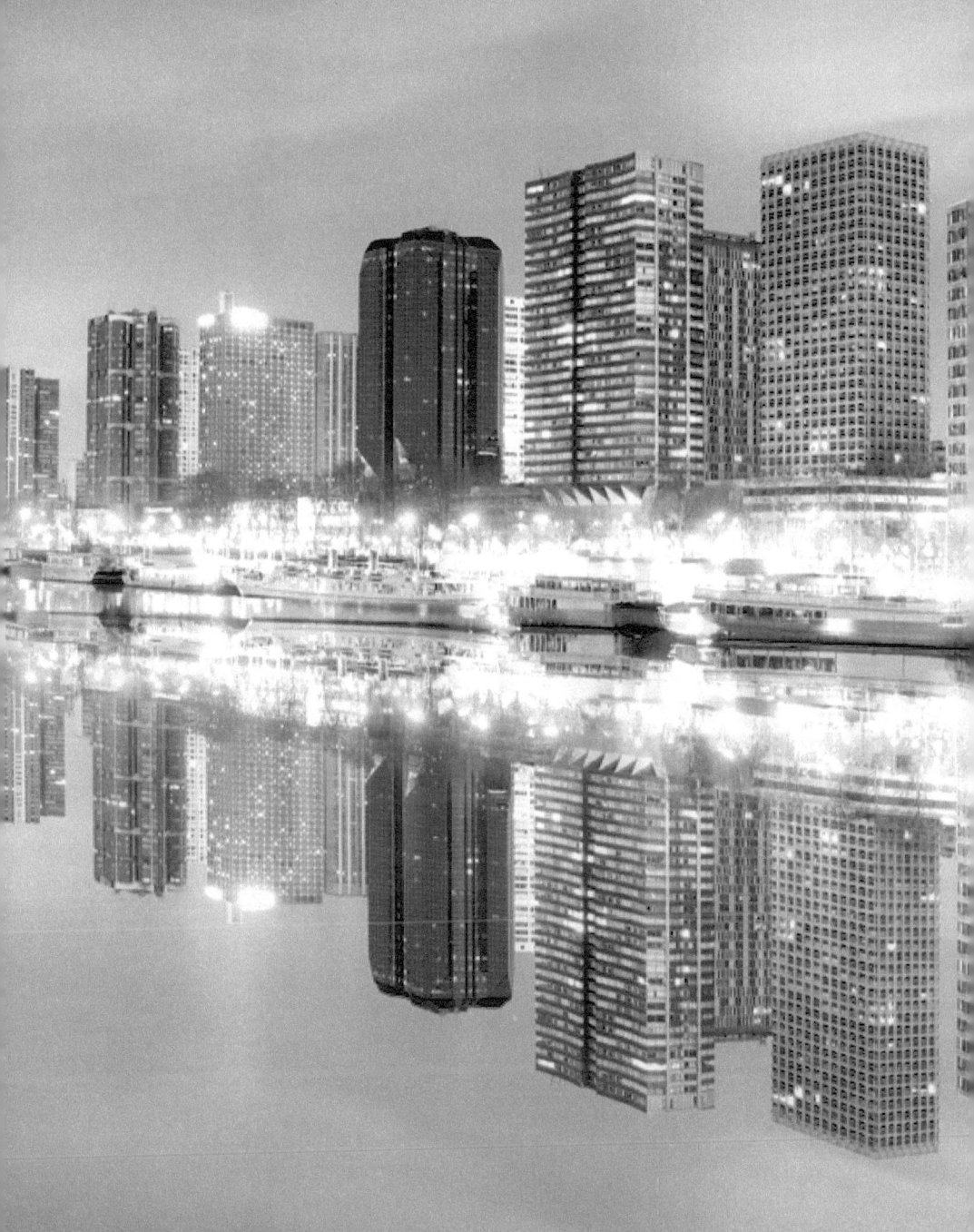

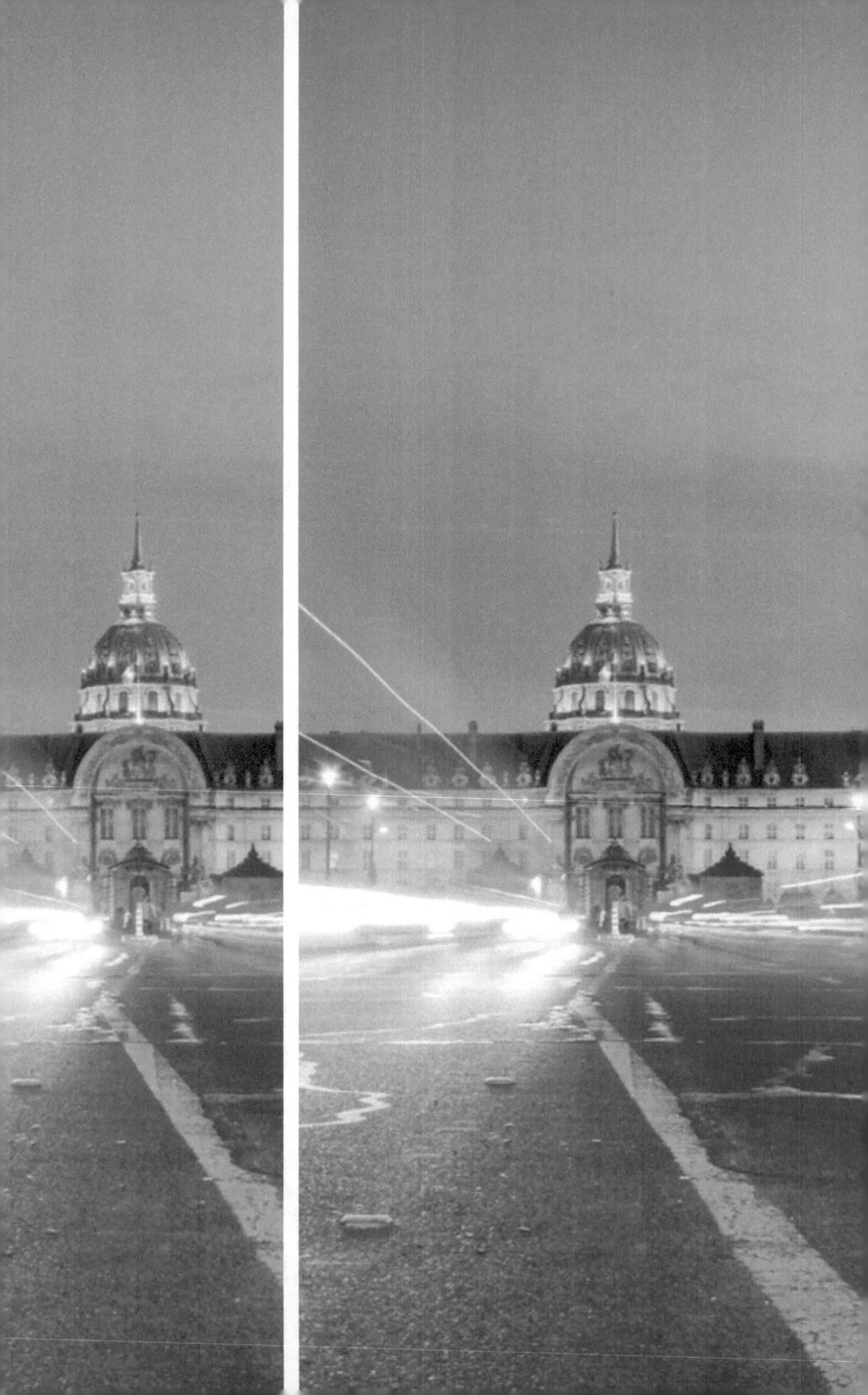

"London is a riddle. Paris is an explanation." - G. K. Chesterson

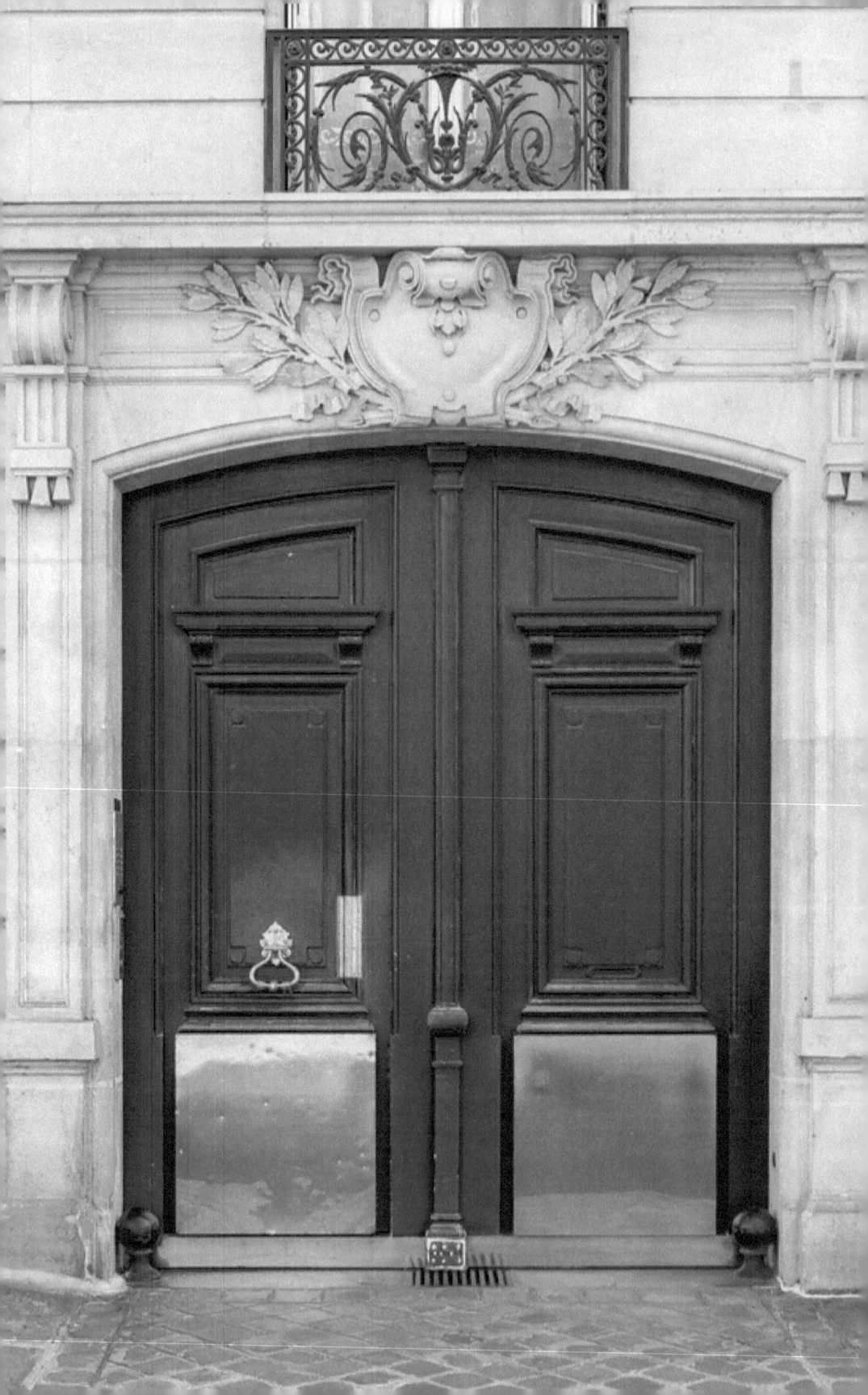

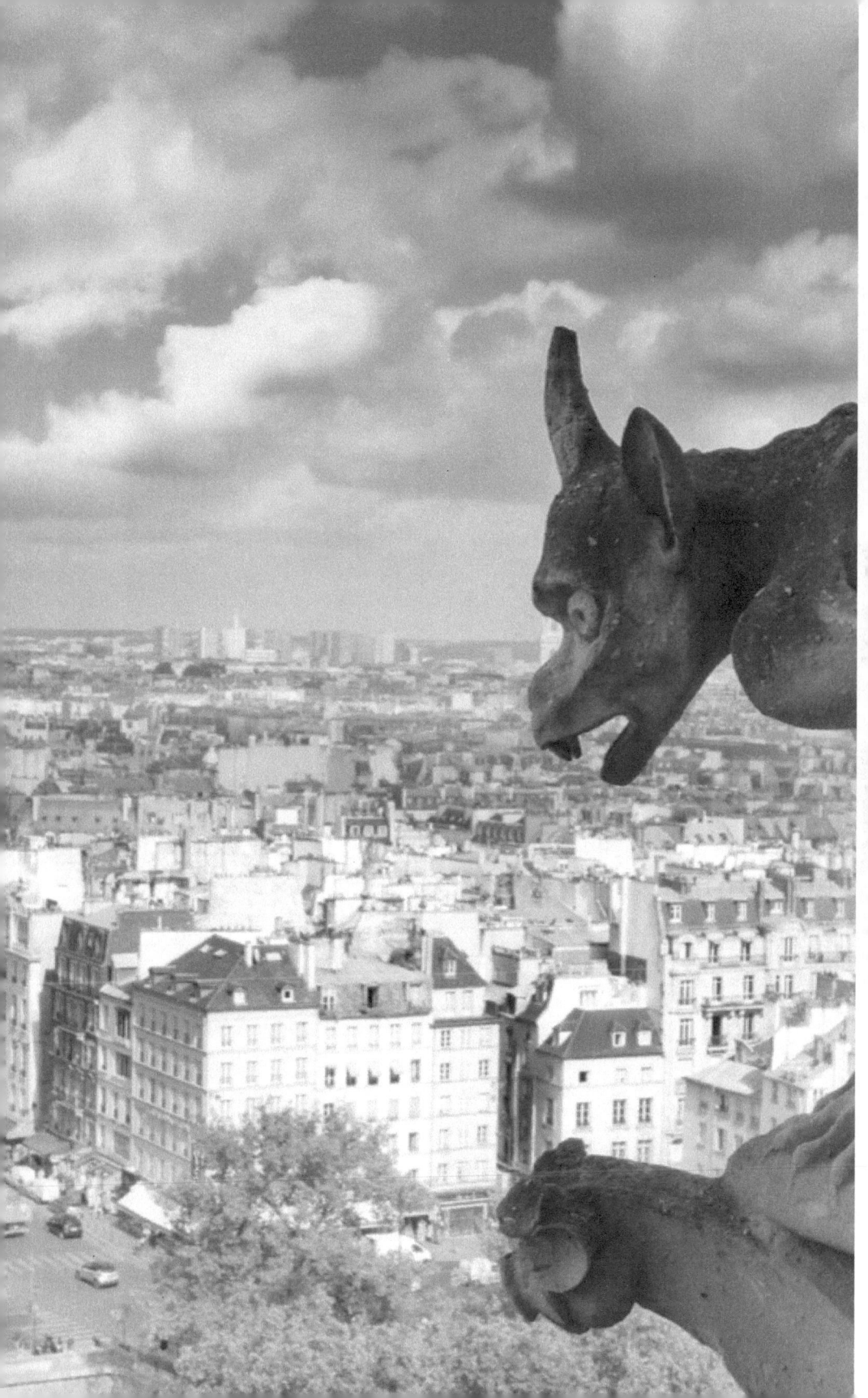

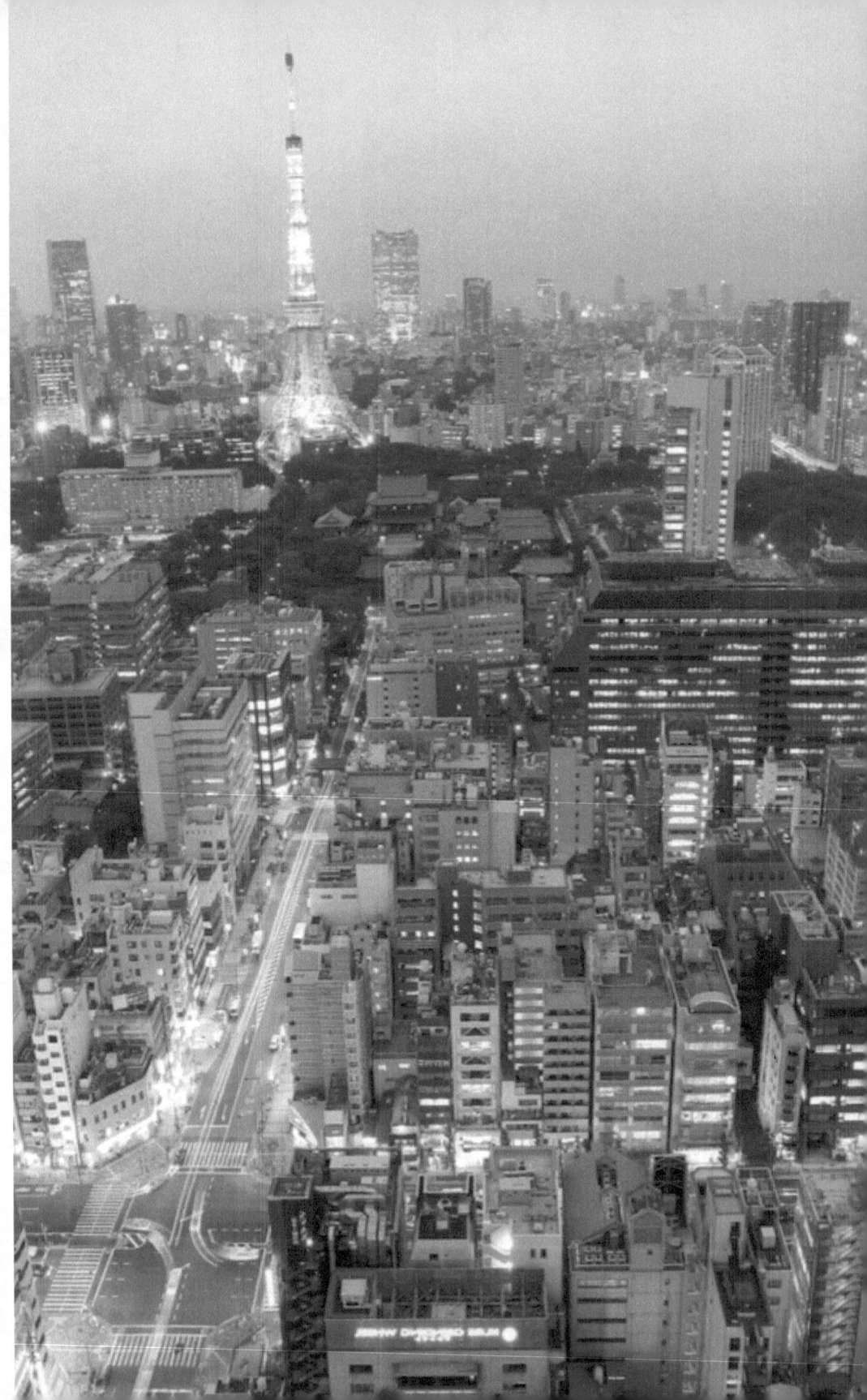

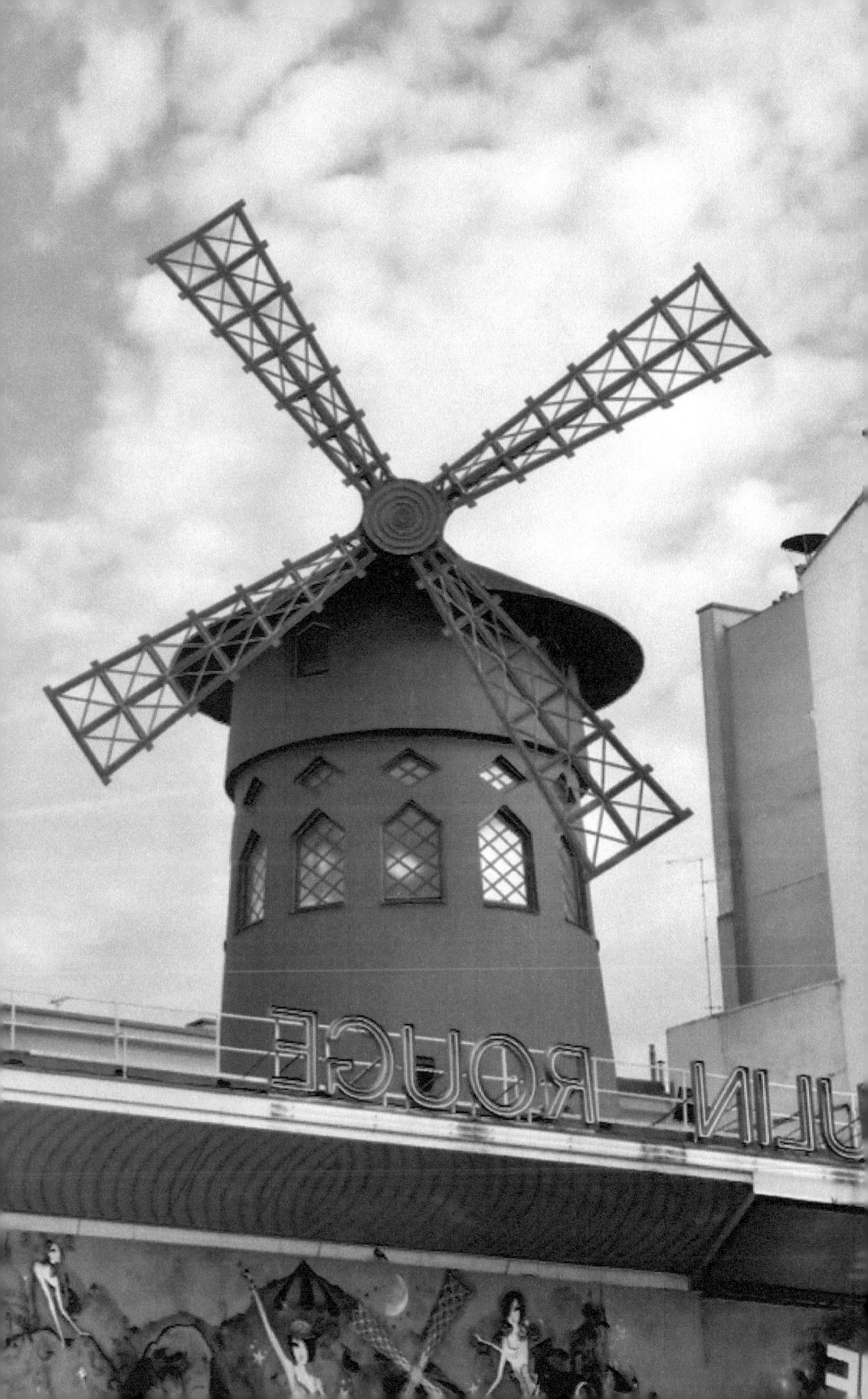

"We'll always have Paris."
Howard Koch

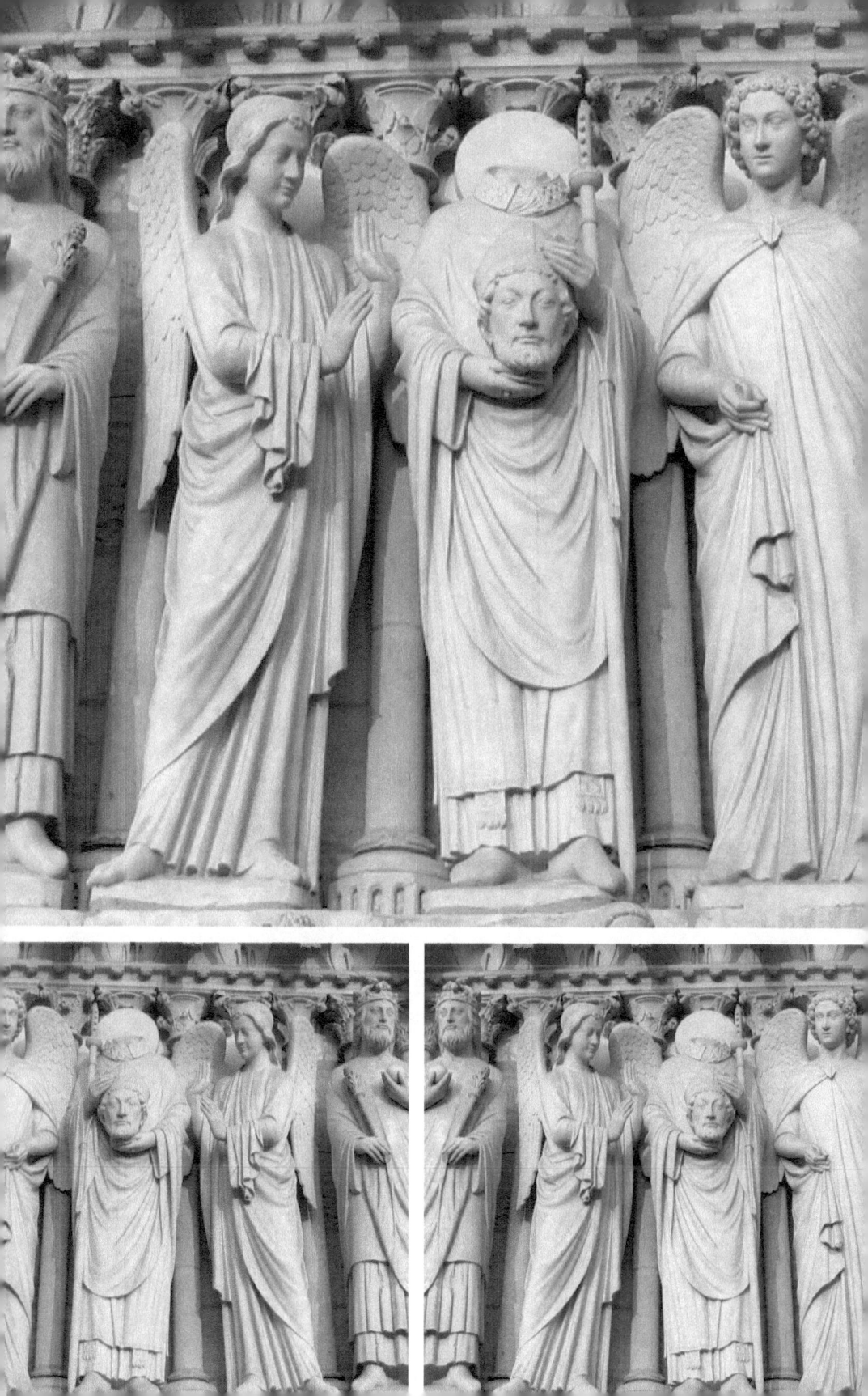

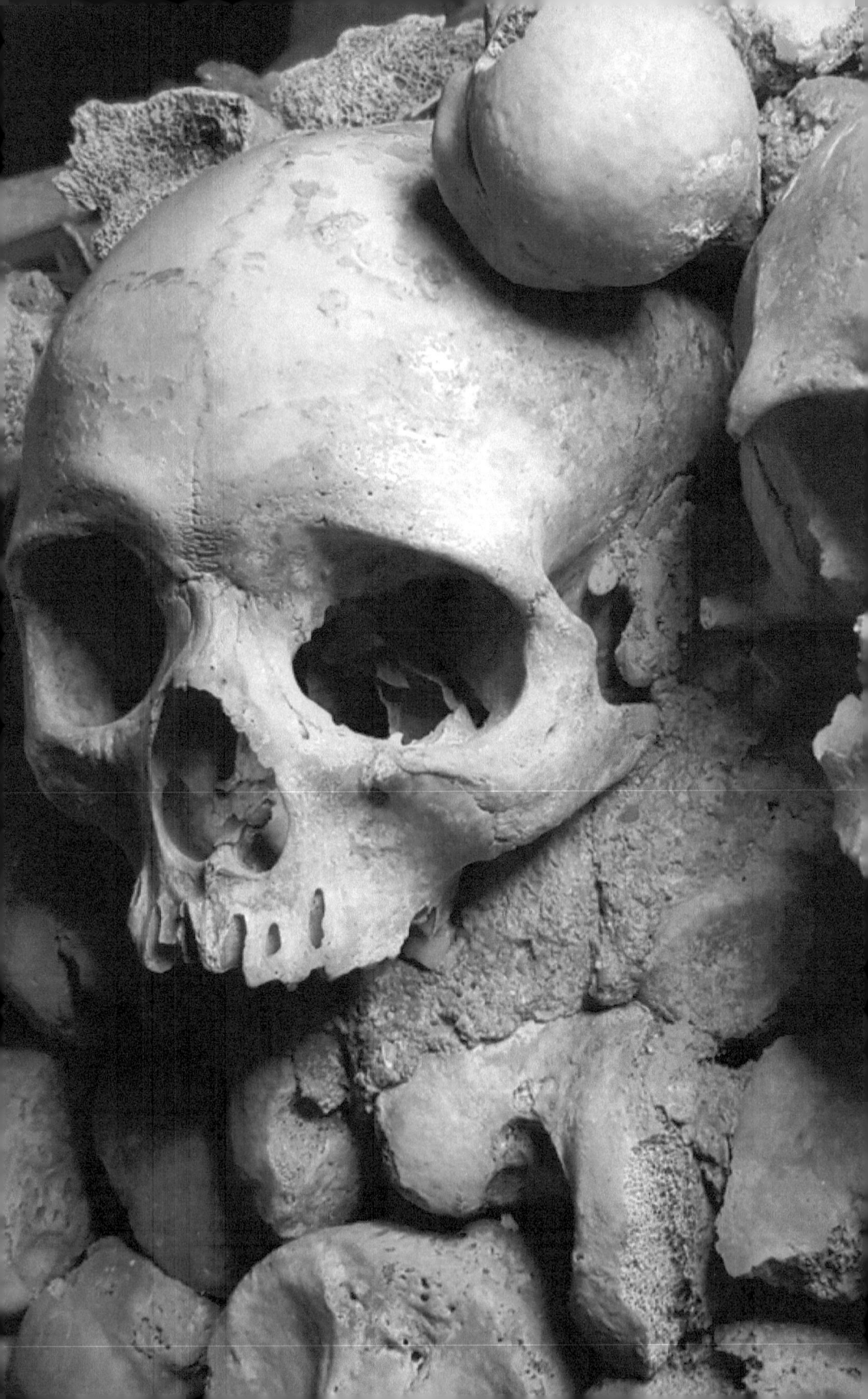

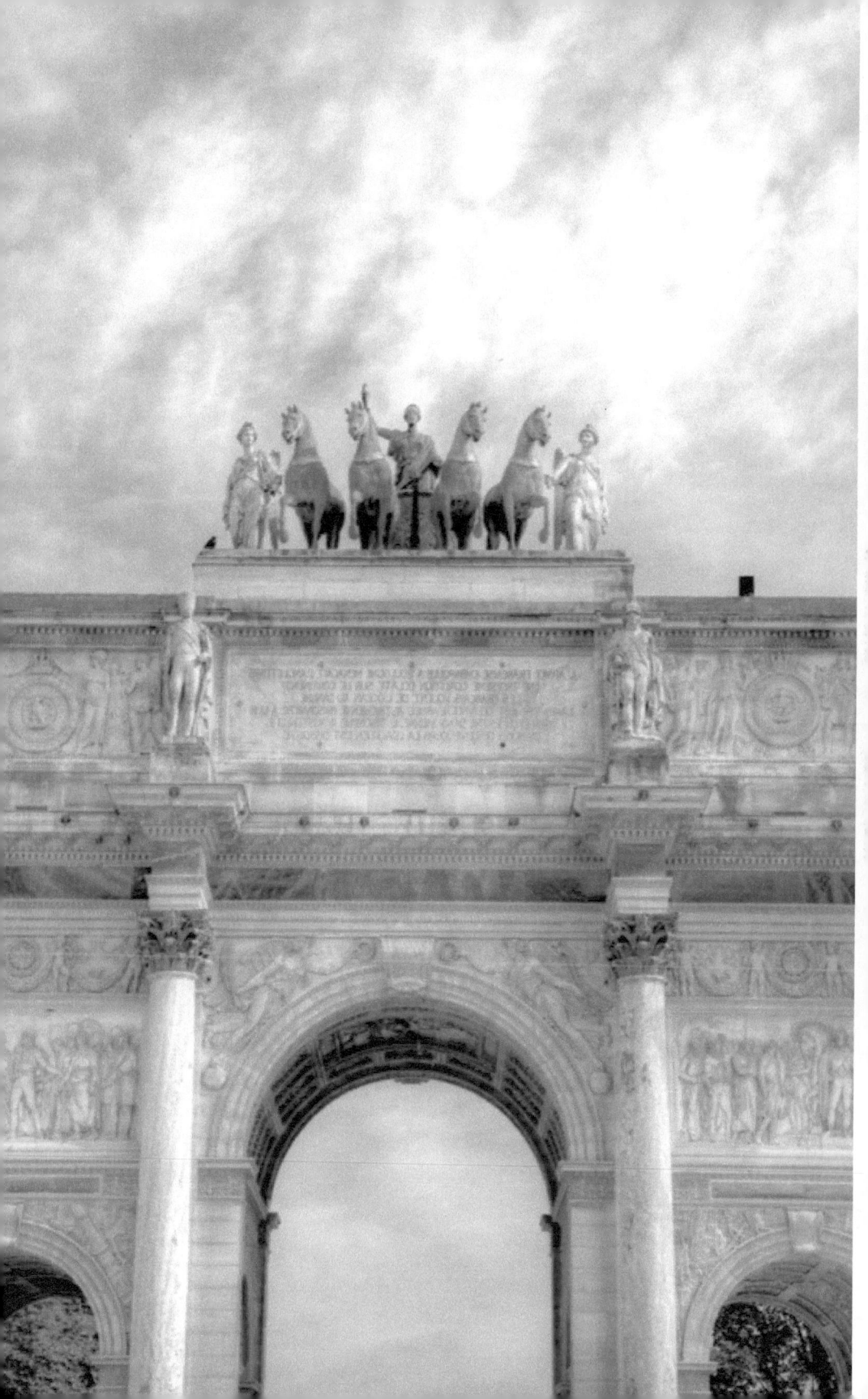

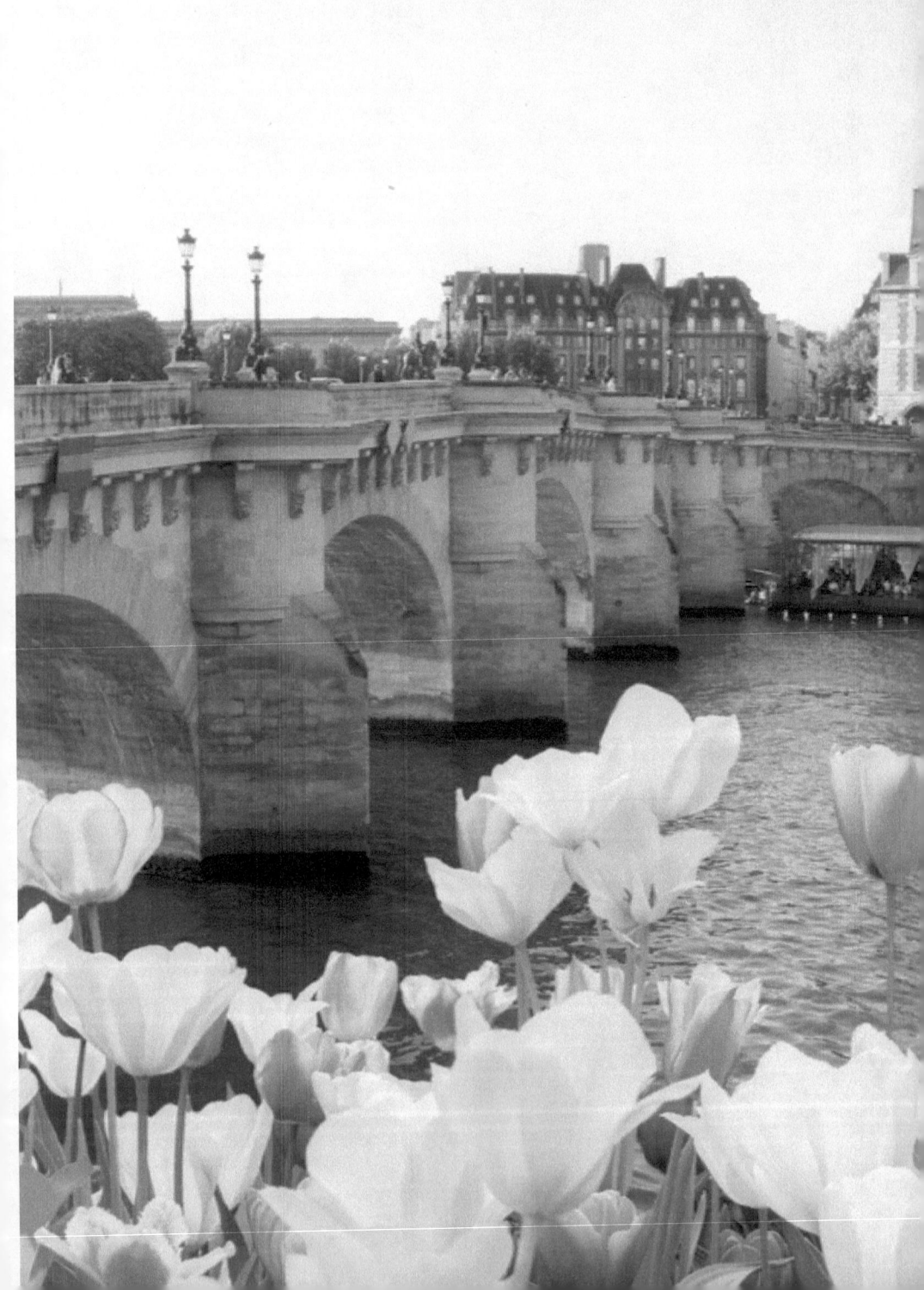

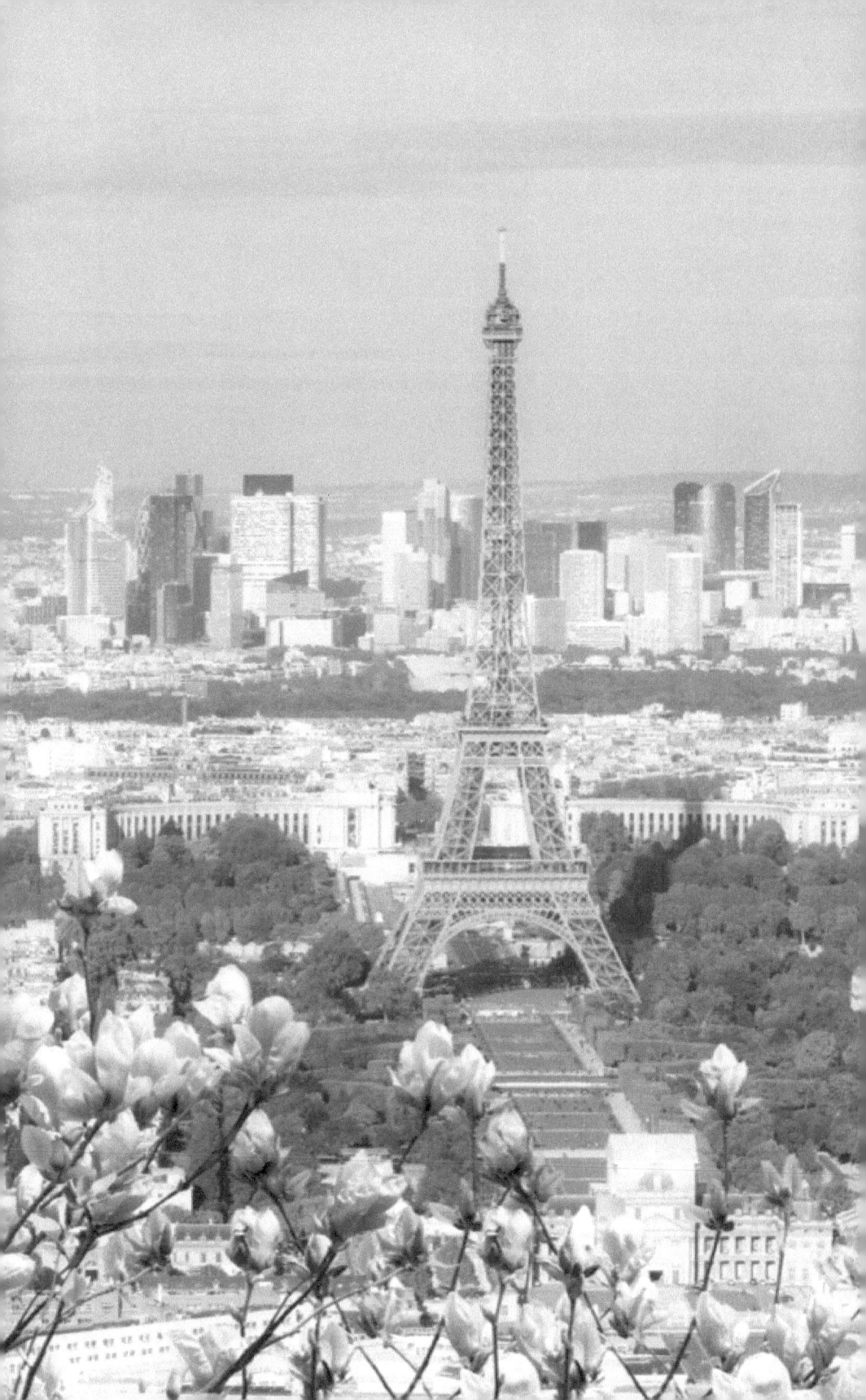

www.ingramcontent.com/pod-product-compliance
Lightning Source LLC
Chambersburg PA
CBHW021036180526
45163CB00005B/2146